Data Warehouse Requirements Engineering

Naveen Prakash · Deepika Prakash

Data Warehouse Requirements Engineering

A Decision Based Approach

 Springer

Naveen Prakash
ICLC Ltd.
New Delhi
India

Deepika Prakash
Central University of Rajasthan
Kishangarh
India

ISBN 978-981-13-4987-4   ISBN 978-981-10-7019-8   (eBook)
https://doi.org/10.1007/978-981-10-7019-8

Printed on acid-free paper

This Springer imprint is published by the registered company Springer Nature Singapore Pte Ltd. part
of Springer Nature.
The registered company address is: 152 Beach Road, #21-01/04 Gateway East, Singapore 189721, Singapore

To
Our Family

Preface

That requirements engineering is part of the systems development life cycle and is about the first activity to be carried out when building systems is today considered as basic knowledge in computer science/information technology. Requirements engineering produces requirements specifications that are carried through to system design and implementation. It is assumed that systems automate specific activities that are carried out in the real world. These activities are transactions, for example reservations, cancellations, buying, selling, and the like. Thus requirements engineering produces requirements specifications of transactional systems.

So long as systems were not very complex, the preparation of a requirements specification was feasible and did not compromise on system delivery times. However, as systems became more and more complex, iterative and incremental development came to the fore. Producing a requirements specification is now frowned upon and we need to produce, in the language of Scrum, user stories for small parts of the system.

About the time requirements engineering was developing, data warehousing also became important. Data warehouse development faced the same challenges as transactional systems do, namely determination of the requirements to be met and the role of requirements engineering in the era of agile development. However, both these issues have been taken up relatively recently.

Due to this recent interest in the area, requirements engineering for data warehousing is relatively unknown. We fear that there is widespread paucity of understanding of the nature of data warehouse requirements engineering, how it differs from traditional transaction-oriented requirements engineering and what are the new issues that it raises.

Perhaps, the role of agility in data warehouse development is even more crucial than in transactional systems development. This is because of the inherent complexity of data warehouse systems, long lead times to delivery, and the huge costs involved in their development. Indeed, the notion of data marts and the bus approach to data warehouse development is an early response to these challenges.

This book is our attempt at providing exposure to the problem of data warehouse requirements engineering. We hope that the book shall contribute to a wider awareness of the difference between requirements engineering for transactional and data warehouse systems, and of the challenges that data warehousing presents to the requirements engineering community.

The position adopted in this book is that even in the face of agile development, requirements engineering continues to be relevant. Requirements engineering today is not to produce requirements specifications of entire systems. Rather, it is done to support incremental and iterative development. In other words, rather than restrict incremental and iterative development to downstream tasks of design and implementation, we must extend it to the requirements engineering task as well. We argue that the entire data warehouse systems development life cycle should become agile.

Thus, we make requirements and requirements engineering as the fulcrum for data warehouse agile development. Just as requirements specifications *of systems* formed the basis for proceeding with systems development earlier, so also now requirements specifications *of system increments* must form the basis of incremental and iterative development.

Following this line of argument, instead of a requirements specification, we propose to develop requirements granules. It is possible to consider building a requirements granule per data mart. However, we consider a data mart as having very large granularity because it addresses an entire subject like sales, purchase etc. Therefore, the requirements granule that will be produced shall be large-grained resulting in relatively long lead times to delivery of the intended product increment. It is worth developing an approach to requirements engineering that can produce requirements granules of smaller sizes.

To reduce the sizes of requirements granules, we introduce the notion of a decision and propose to build data warehouse fragments for decisions. Thus, data warehouse requirements engineering is for discovering the decisions of interest and then determining the information relevant to each decision. A requirements granule is the collection of information relevant to a decision. If this information is available then it is possible for the decision maker to obtain it from the data warehouse fragment, evaluate it, and decide whether to take the decision or not. This implies that the size of a granule is determined by the amount of information that is associated with a decision.

The notion of a decision is thus central to our approach. A decision represents the useful work that the data warehouse fragment supports and a data warehouse fragment is the implementation of a requirements fragment. The approach in this book represents a departure from the conventional notion of a data mart that is built to "analyze" a subject area. Analysis for us is not an aim in itself but taking a decision is and analysis is only in support of the decision making task.

As more and more decisions are taken up for development, there is a proliferation of requirements granules and data warehouse fragments. This results in problems of inconsistent information across the enterprise, and of proliferating costs due to multiple platforms and ETL processes. This is similar to what happens in the bus-of-data-marts approach except that a decision may be of a lower granularity than a data mart. This means that we can expect many more data warehouse fragments than data marts and the problem of inconsistency and costs is even more severe.

Given the severity of the problem, we do not consider it advisable to wait for the problem to appear and then take corrective action by doing consolidation. It is best to take a preventive approach that minimizes fragment proliferation. Again, keeping in mind that for us requirements are the fulcrum for data warehouse development, we consolidate requirements granules even as they are defined.

This book is a summary of research in the area of data warehouse requirements engineering carried out by the authors. To be sure, this research is ongoing and we expect to produce some more interesting results in the future. However, we believe that we have reached a point where the results we have achieved form a coherent whole from which the research and industrial community can benefit.

The initial three chapters of the book form the backdrop for the last three. We devote Chap. 1 to the state of the art in transactional requirement engineering whereas Chap. 2 is for data warehouse requirements engineering. The salient issues in data warehouse requirements engineering addressed in this book are presented in Chap. 3.

Chapter 4 deals with the different types of decisions and contains techniques for their elicitation. Chapter 5 is devoted to information elicitation for decisions and the basic notion of a requirements granule is formulated here. Chapter 6 deals with agility built around the idea of the requirements granules and data warehouse fragments. The approach to data warehouse consolidation is explained here.

The book can be used in two ways. For those readers interested in a broad-brush understanding of the differences between transactional and data warehouse requirements engineering, the first three chapters would suffice. However, for those interested in deeper knowledge, the rest of the chapters would be of relevance as well.

New Delhi, India   Naveen Prakash
Kishangarh, India   Deepika Prakash
September 2017

Contents

About the Authors

Naveen Prakash started his career with the Computer Group of Bhabha Atomic Research Centre Mumbai in 1972. He obtained his doctoral degree from the Indian Institute of Technology Delhi (IIT Delhi) in 1980. He subsequently worked at the National Center for Software Development and Computing Techniques, Tata Institute of Fundamental Research (NCSDCT, TIFR) before joining the R&D group of CMC Ltd where he worked for over 10 years doing industrial R&D. In 1989, he moved to academics. He worked at the Department of Computer Science and Engineering, Indian Institute of Technology Kanpur (IIT Kanpur), and at the Delhi Institute of Technology (DIT) (now Netaji Subhas Institute of Technology (NSIT)), Delhi. During this period he provided consultancy services to Asian Development Bank and African Development Bank projects in Sri Lanka and Tanzania, respectively, as well as to the Indira Gandhi National Centre for the Arts (IGNCA) as a United Nations Development Programme (UNDP) consultant. He served as a scientific advisor to the British Council Division, New Delhi and took up the directorship of various educational institutes in India. Post-retirement, he worked on a World Bank project in Malawi.

Prof. Prakash has lectured extensively in various universities abroad. He is on the editorial board of the Requirements Engineering Journal, and of the International Journal of Information System Modeling and Design (IJISMD). He has published over 70 research papers and authored two books.

Prof. Prakash continues to be an active researcher. Besides Business Intelligence and Data Warehousing, his interests include the Internet-of-things and NoSQL database. He also lectures at the Indira Gandhi Delhi Technical University for Women (IGDTUW), Delhi and IIIT Delhi.

Deepika Prakash obtained her Ph.D. from Delhi Technological University, Delhi in the area of Data Warehouse Requirements Engineering. Currently, she is an Assistant Professor at the Department of Big Data Analytics, Central University of Rajasthan, Rajasthan.

Dr. Prakash has five years of teaching experience, as well as two years of experience in industrial R&D, building data marts for purchase, sales and inventory and in data mart integration. Her responsibilities in industry spanned the complete life cycle, from requirements engineering through conceptual modeling to extract-transform-load (ETL) activities.

As a researcher, she has authored a number of papers in international forums and has delivered invited lectures at a number of Institutes throughout India. Her current research interests include Business Intelligence, Health Analytics, and the Internet-of-Things.

Chapter 1
Requirements Engineering for Transactional Systems

Transactional systems have been the forte of Information Systems/Software Engineering. These systems deal with automating the functionality of systems, to provide value to the users. Initially, up to the end of the decade of the 1960s, transactional systems were simple, single-function systems. Thus, we had payroll systems that accounts people would use to compute the salary of employees and print out salary. Information Systems/Software Engineering technology graduated to multi-functional systems that looked at the computerization of relatively larger chunks of the business. Thus, it now became possible to deal with the accounts department, the human resource department, customer interface, etc. Technology to deal with such systems stabilized in the period 1960–1980. Subsequently, attention shifted to even more complex systems, the computerization of the entire enterprise, and to inter-organization information systems.

The demand for engineering of ever more complex systems led to the "software crisis", a term widely used in the 1990s to describe the difficulties that industry of that time faced. A number of studies were carried out and some of the problems highlighted were systems failure/rejection by clients, inability to deliver complex and large software well.

The Standish Group's "Chaos" reports [1] presented software industry's record in delivering large-sized systems using traditional development methods. The Group conducted a survey of 8380 projects carried out by 365 major American companies. The results showed that projects worth up to even $750,000 exceeded budget and time. Further, they failed to deliver the promised features more than 55% of the time. As the size of the applications grew, the success rate fell to 25% for efforts over $3 million and down to zero for projects over $10 million.

Bell labs and IBM [2] found that 80% of all defects in software products lie in the requirements phase. Boehm and Papaccio [3] said that correcting requirements errors is 5 times more expensive when carried out during the design phase; the cost of correction is 10 times during implementation phase; the cost rises to 20 times for corrections done during testing and it becomes an astronomical 200 times after the system has been delivered. Evidently, such corrections result in expensive products

© Springer Nature Singapore Pte Ltd. 2018
N. Prakash and D. Prakash, *Data Warehouse Requirements Engineering*,
https://doi.org/10.1007/978-981-10-7019-8_1

and/or total rejection of software. The Standish group [4] reported that one of the reasons for project failure is "incomplete requirements". Clearly, the effect of poorly engineered requirements ranges from outright systems rejection by the customer to major reworking of the developed system.

The *Software Hall of Shame* [5] surveyed around 30 large software development projects that failed between 1992 and 2005 to try to identify the causes of this failure. It was found that failures arise because either projects go beyond actual needs or because of expansion in the scope of the original project. This implied that requirements changed over the course of product development and this change was difficult to handle.

The foregoing suggested that new methods of software development were needed that delivered on time, on budget, met their requirements, and were also capable of handling changing requirements. The response was twofold:

- An emphasis on incremental and iterative product development rather than one-shot development of the entire product. Small, carefully selected product parts were developed and integrated with other parts as and when these latter became available. As we shall see this took the form of agile software development.
- The birth of the discipline of requirements engineering in which the earlier informal methods were replaced by model-driven methods. This led to the systematization of the requirements engineering process, computer-based management of requirements, guidance in the requirements engineering task, and so on.

We discuss these two responses in the rest of this chapter.

1.1   Transactional System Development Life Cycle

The System Development Life cycle, SDLC, for transactional systems (TSDLC) starts from gathering system/software requirements and ends with the deployment of the system. One of the earliest models of TSDLC is the waterfall model. The waterfall model has six sequential phases. Each phase has different actors participating in it. Output of one phase forms the input to the next phase. This output is documented and used by the actors of the next phase. The size of documentation produced is very large and time-consuming.

Since the model is heavy on documentation, the model is sometimes referred to as document driven. Table 1.1 shows the actors and document produced against each phase of the life cycle.

The process starts with identifying what needs to be built. There are usually several stakeholders of a system. Each stakeholder sits down with the requirements engineer and details what s/he specifically expects from the system. These needs are referred to as requirements. A more formal definition of the term requirements is available in the subsequent sections of this chapter. These requirements as given

Table 1.1 The different phases of TSDLC

TSDLC phase	Actor	Document
Requirements engineering	Stakeholder, Requirements engineer	System requirements specification
System and software design	System analysts	High-level and low-level design documents
Implementation	Development team	Code
Verification	Tester	Test case document
Maintenance	Project manager, Stakeholder	User manuals

by the stakeholder are documented as a System Requirements Specification (SRS) document.

Once the SRS is produced, the actors of the system design phase, system analyst, convert the requirements into high-level design and low-level design. The former describes the software architecture. The latter discusses the data structure to be used, the interfaces and other procedural details. Here, two documents are produced, the high-level and low-level design document.

The design documents are made available to the implementation team for the development activity to start. Apart from development, unit testing is also a feature of this phase. In the Verification phase, functional and non-functional testing is performed and a detailed test case document is produced. Often test cases are designed with involvement of the stakeholders. Thus, apart from the testers, stakeholders are also actors of this phase. Finally, the software is deployed and support is provided for maintenance of the product.

Notice, each phase is explored fully before moving on to the next phase. Also notice, there is no feedback path to go to a previous already completed phase. Consider the following scenario. The product is in the implementation phase and the developers realize that an artifact has been poorly conceptualized. In other words, there is a need to rework a part of the conceptual model for development to proceed. However, there is no provision in the model to go back to the system design phase once the product is in the development phase.

This model also implies that

(a) Requirements once specified do not change. However, this is rarely the case. A feedback path is required in the event of changing requirements. This ensures that changes are incorporated in the current software release rather than waiting for the next release to adopt the changed requirement.
(b) "All" requirements can be elicited from the stakeholders. The requirements engineering phase ends with a sign-off from the stakeholder. However, as already brought out, studies have shown that it is not possible to elicit all the requirements upfront from the stakeholders. Stakeholders are often unable to envision changes that could arise 12–24 months down the line and generally mention requirements as of the day of the interview with the requirements engineer.

Being sequential in nature, a working model of the product is released only at the end of the life cycle. This leads to two problems. One that feedback can be got from the stakeholder only after the entire product is developed and delivered. Even a slightly negative feedback means that the entire system has to be redeveloped; considerable time and effort in delivering the product is wasted.

The second problem is that these systems suffer from long lead time for product delivery. This is because the entire requirements specification is made before the system is taken up for design and implementation.

An alternate method to system development is to adopt an agile development model. The aim of this model is to provide an **iterative** and **incremental** development framework for delivery of a product. An iteration is defined by clear deliverables which are identified by the stakeholder. Deliverables are pieces of the product _usable_ by the stakeholder. Several iterations are performed to deliver the final product making the development process incremental. Also, iterations are time boxed with time allocated to each iteration remaining almost the same till the final product is delivered.

One of the popular approaches to agile development is Scrum. In Scrum, iterations are referred to as sprints. There are two actors, product owner and developer. The product owner is the stakeholder of the waterfall model. The requirements are elicited in the form of user stories. A user story is defined as a single sentence that identifies a need. User stories have three parts, "Who" identifies the stakeholder, "What" identifies the action, and "Why" identifies the reason behind the action. A good user story is one that is actionable, meaning that the developer is able to use it to deliver the need at the end of the sprint.

Wake [6] introduced the INVEST test as a measure of how good a user story is. A good user story must meet the following criteria: Independent, Not too specific, Valuable, Estimable, Small, and Testable. One major issue in building stories is that of determining when the story is "small". Small is defined as that piece of work that can be delivered in a sprint. User stories as elicited from the product owner may not fit in a sprint. Scrum uses the epic–theme–user story decomposition approach to deal with this. Epics are stories identified by the product owner in the first conversation. They require several sprints to deliver. In order to decompose the epic, further interaction with the product owner is performed to yield themes. However, a theme by itself may take several sprints, but a lesser number than for its epic, to deliver. Therefore, a theme is further decomposed into user stories of the right size.

When comparing agile development model with the waterfall model, there are two major differences as follows:

1. In Scrum, sprints do not wait for the full requirements specification to be produced. Further, the requirements behind a user story are also not fully specified but follow the 80–20 principle. 80% of the requirements need to be clarified before proceeding with a sprint and the balance 20% are discovered during the sprint. Thus, while in waterfall model, stakeholder involvement in the requirements engineering phase ends with a sign-off from the stakeholder, in Scrum the stakeholder is involved during the entire life cycle. In fact, iterations proceed with the feedback of the stakeholder.

2. At the end of one iteration, a working sub-product is delivered to the stakeholder. This could either be an enhancement or a new artifact. This is unlike the waterfall model where the entire product is delivered at the end of the life cycle.

1.2 Transactional Requirements Engineering

Let us start with some basic definitions that tell us what requirements are and what requirements engineering does.

Requirements

A requirement has been defined in a number of ways. Some definitions are as follows.

Definition 1: A requirement as defined in [7] is *"(1) a condition or capability needed by a user to solve a problem or achieve an objective, (2) A condition or capability that must be met or possessed by a system or system components to satisfy a contract, standard, specification or other formally imposed documents, (3) A document representation of a condition as in (1) or in (2)"*.

According to this definition, requirements arise from user, general organization, standards, government bodies, etc. These requirements are then documented.

A requirement is considered as a specific property of a product by Robertson, and Kotonya as shown in Definition 2 and Definition 3 below.

Definition 2: "Something that the product must do or a quality that the product must have" [8].

Definition 3: "A description of how the system shall behave, and information about the application domain, constraints on operations, a system property etc." [9].

Definition 4: "Requirements are high level abstractions of the services the system shall provide and the constraints imposed on the system".

Requirements have been classified as functional requirements, FR, and non-functional requirements, NFR. Functional requirements are "statements about what a system should do, how it should behave, what it should contain, or what components it should have" and non-functional requirements are "statements of quality, performance and environment issues with which the system should conform" [10]. Non-functional requirements are global qualities of a software system, such as flexibility, maintainability, etc. [11].

Requirements Engineering

Requirements engineering, RE, is the process of obtaining and modeling requirements. Indeed, a number of definitions of RE exist in literature.

Definition 1: Requirements engineering (RE) is defined [7] as *"the systemic process of developing requirements through an iterative cooperative process of analyzing* *the problem, documenting the resulting observations in a variety of representation formats and checking the accuracy of understanding gained*".

The process is cooperative because different stakeholders have different needs and therefore varying viewpoints. RE must take into account conflicting views and interests of users and stakeholders. Capturing different viewpoints allows conflicts to surface at an early stage in the requirements process. Further, the resulting requirements are the ones that are agreeable to both customers and developers.

Definition 2 Zave [12]: Requirements engineering deals with the real-world goals for functions and constraints of the software system. It makes a precise specification of software behavior and its evolution over time.

This definition incorporates "real-world goals" in its definition. In other words, this definition hopes to capture requirements that answer the "why" of software systems. Here, the author is referring to "functional requirements". Further, the definition also gives emphasis to "precise requirements". Thus quality of requirements captured is also important.

Definition 3 van Lamsweerde [13]: RE deals with the identification of goals to be achieved by the system to be developed, the operationalization of such goals into services and constraints.

Definition 4 Nuseibeh and Easterbrook [14]: RE aims to discover the purpose behind the system to be built, by identifying stakeholders and their needs, and their documentation.

Here, the emphasis is on *identifying stakeholders* and capturing the requirements of the stakeholders.

1.3   Requirements Engineering (RE) as a Process

Evidently, requirements engineering can be viewed as a process with an input and an output. Stakeholders are the problem owners. They can be users, designers, system analysts, business analysts, technical authors, and customers. In the RE process, requirements are elicited from these sources. Output of the process is generally a set of agreed requirements, system specifications, and system models. The first two of these are in the form of use cases, goals, agents, or NFRs. System models can be object models, goal models, domain descriptions, behavioral models, problem frames, etc.

There are three fundamental concerns of RE, namely, understanding the problem, describing the problem, and attaining an agreement on the nature of the problem. The process involves several actors for the various activities. We visualize the entire process as shown in Fig. 1.1. There are four stages each with specific actors, marked with green in the figure. A requirements engineer is central in the entire process.

Let us elaborate the components of the figure.

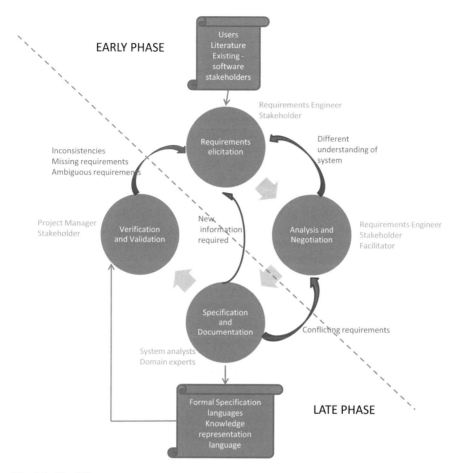

Fig. 1.1 The RE process

"**Requirements Elicitation**": Requirements are elicited from users, domain experts, literature, and existing software that is similar to the one to be built, stakeholders, etc. As can be seen in the figure, this forms the input into this step. The actors involved in this step are requirements engineer and stakeholders. The requirements engineer uses one or more of the several elicitation techniques, described in the later sections of this chapter, elicits requirements from the stakeholder. Usually, several sessions are required where each session may employ a different elicitation technique. This is a labor-intensive step and usually takes a large amount of time and resources.

"**Analysis/Negotiation**": Requirements elicited during the previous step is input into this step. As can be seen in the figure, a facilitator is also an actor along with requirements engineer and stakeholders. There are multiple stakeholders for the systems to-be. Each stakeholder may have a different view of what functionality the system must have and what is the goal of building the system to-be. This gives rise to conflicts. In this step, an agreement between the various stakeholders on the requirements of the system to-be is established with the help of a facilitator. Notice a red arrow in Fig. 1.1 from this step to the previous requirements elicitation step. It may happen that during resolution of the conflicts, there is a new and different understanding of the system entirely or of a part of the system. By going back to the requirements elicitation stage, new requirements are elicited.

"**Specification** and **Documentation**": Once all conflicts are resolved, requirements are documented for use in subsequent stages of system development. As shown in Fig. 1.1, the document may be in formal specification languages, knowledge representation languages, etc. System analyst and domain experts are involved in this task. It is possible that during documentation new conflicting requirements are found. To accommodate this, there is a feedback loop, shown by the red arrow, which goes from this stage to the "analysis/negotiation" stage. It may also happen that more information in the form of requirements is needed for the system to be built. For this, there is a loop (red arrow in the figure) to the "requirements specification" stage.

"**Verification** and **Validation**" (**V&V**): The main goal here is to check if the document meets the customers'/clients' needs. The input into this stage is the documented requirements. The project manager along with the stakeholder is involved in this task. Consistency and completeness are some aspects of the document that are checked. Once the requirements have been verified and validated, the RE process is considered completed and other phases of the TSDLC described in Sect. 1.1 are executed. However, if any inconsistencies, missing requirements or ambiguous requirements are found, then the entire process is repeated.

There are two phases of RE, an early phase and late RE phase. The dotted line running diagonally across Fig. 1.1 divides the RE process into the two phases. Early RE phase focuses on whether the interest of stakeholders is being addressed or compromised. Requirements elicitation and analysis/negotiation form the early RE phase. Late RE phase focuses on consistency, completeness, and verification of requirements [15].

1.4 Informal Approaches to Requirements Elicitation

Requirements elicitation was initially performed using techniques like interviews, analyzing existing documentation, questionnaires group elicitation techniques, brainstorming, and eventually evolved into JAD/RAD, workshops, prototyping, contextual, cognitive, and ethnographic studies. This set of techniques is "informal", in contrast to model-driven techniques described later.

Let us look at each of these approaches individually, in terms of the technique employed to elicit requirements, their advantages and disadvantages.

 (i) **Interviews**—Interviews are held between the requirements engineer and the stakeholder. Interviews are commonly acknowledged to be a stimulus–response interaction [16]. This interaction is based on some (usually unstated) assumptions [16]. The requirements engineer prepares a set of "relevant questions" in order to get to know what the stakeholders want. It is assumed that the questions will be read without variation, will be interpreted in an unambiguous way, and will stimulate a valid response. Suchman and Jordan [17] argue that this validity is not assured. There is another problem of the requirements engineer trying to impose their views in the form of the questions they ask.

 (ii) **Analyzing existing documentation**—Documentation like organizational charts, process models, or standards or existing manuals can be analyzed to gather requirements for systems that closely resemble or are a replacement to an old system. If the documentation is well done, then it can form a rich source of requirements [10]. Great caution has to be imposed while analyzing the documentation. A tendency to over-analyze the existing documentation often leads to the new system to be too constrained [18].

(iii) **Questionnaires**—This technique is generally used for problems that are fairly concrete and in understanding the external needs of a customer [18]. This method has several advantages. One can, quickly collect information from large numbers of people, administer it remotely, and can collect attitudes, beliefs, and characteristics of the customer. However, this technique has certain disadvantages [16]. The questionnaire can have simplistic (presupposed) categories providing very little context. It also limits room for users to convey their real needs. One must also be careful while selecting the sample to prevent any bias.

 (iv) **Group elicitation techniques**—Focus groups are a kind of group interviews [16]. They overcome the problem of the interviewing technique being a very rigid interaction. This technique exploits the fact that a more natural interaction between people helps elicit richer needs [14]. The groups generally are formed ad hoc based on the agenda of the day. It usually consists of stakeholders and requirements engineers. These group elicitation techniques are good for uncovering responses to products. These techniques overcome the disadvantages of interviews. However, they are not found to be effective in uncovering design requirements. Two popular groups are the Joint Application Development (JAD) and the Rapid Application Development (RAD) group.

 (v) **Brainstorming**—[19] This is highly specialized groups consisting of actual users, middle level, and/or total stakeholders brainstorm in order to elicit the requirements. This process has two phases: idea *generation* and idea *reduction*. In the idea generation phase, many ideas as possible are generated. These ideas are then mutated. Ideas can also be combined. The idea reduction phase involves pruning ideas generated in the idea generation phase that are not worthy of further discussion. Similar ideas are grouped into one super topic. The ideas that survive the idea reduction phase are documented and prioritized. There is a trained facilitator during both the phases. The job of this facilitator is to see to it that criticism and personal egos of the group members do not come into play. He/she should also ensure that a published agenda is strictly followed.

(vi) **Workshops**—This is one of the most powerful techniques for eliciting requirements [19]. Workshops are attended by all key stakeholders for a short but intensely focused period. Brainstorming is the most important part of the workshop [14]. It is agenda based. The agenda is published along with the other pre-workshop documentation. Balance is the key to workshops. There is an outside facilitator to see that the group tries to follow the agenda but to not to strictly obey it, especially if good discussion is going on.

(vii) **Prototyping**—This technique has been used where requirements are uncertain or fuzzy or when customer feedback is required [14]. Here, tangible operating subsystems are built and feedback is sought from the customers. Prototyping is generally combined with other elicitation techniques. Building prototypes are useful when the system to be built is small and the cost of prototyping is low. An additional constraint is that rapid prototyping should not be done unless building the subsystem is really rapid [18]. Prototyping is proposed for exploring the friendliness of user interfaces, thus helping in converting a vague goal like "user friendliness" into specific system properties or behavior.

(viii) **Contextual**—Software systems are used in a social and organizational context. This can influence or even dominate the system requirements. So it is necessary to determine the requirements corresponding to the social system [20]. For example, consider a hospital procedure for treatment of patients. In India, the hospital first asks for the patient to register. However, in Europe the first thing asked is for insurance coverage. Therefore, the system designed for an Indian hospital will have a different set of requirements. Another example of booking a ticket can be looked at. In India, we first block a seat and then pay. However, in Europe payment has to be made before blocking the seat. To capture this social and organizational context, a social scientist observes and analyzes how people actually work.

(ix) **Cognitive-Knowledge elicitation techniques**—Knowledge related to the domain and performance can be elicited by this technique [21].

- Eliciting Performance Knowledge. This is done by a procedure called Protocol Analysis. In this method, the experts think aloud. There is an observer who observes the expert and tries to understand the cognitive process of the expert. This method of analysis is good for understanding interaction problems with existing systems.
- Eliciting Domain Knowledge

  (a) Laddering—Probes are used to elicit structure and content of stakeholder knowledge.

(b) Card Sorting—Cards have some domain entity. Stakeholders sort the cards into groups. This technique helps elicit requirements based on some classification knowledge.

- Multiple Experts: Delphi technique—Used where contact between experts is difficult. Each expert submits her judgment. All judgments circulated anonymously. Each expert submits revised judgment. The process iterates.

1.5 Model-Driven Techniques

Informal techniques rely heavily on the intuition of requirements engineer and depend on stakeholders' views. The nature of the questions to be asked, the depth to which a question is to be answered, and the information to be elicited all lie in the minds of the requirements engineer. There is little computer-based support to manage elicited requirements or to guide the requirements engineer in the RE task. Further, as we move to systems with increasing complexity, requirements reflect only the data and processes needed by the system to-be, thereby making it difficult to understand requirements with respect to high-level concerns [22] of the business.

Modeling requirements has today become a core process in requirements elicitation. Generally, the system and possible alternate configurations of the system are modeled. These techniques shift the focus from "what" feature of the system to "why" of the system [23]. While the former focuses on activities of the system, the latter focuses on the rationale for setting the system up. There are two techniques: goals and agent-oriented modeling both of which are interrelated.

1.5.1 Goal Orientation

"Goal-oriented requirements engineering (GORE) is concerned with the use of goals for eliciting, elaborating, structuring, specifying, analyzing, negotiating, documenting, and modifying requirements" [24]. This indicates that goals can be used in almost every activity of the requirements process. Goals have been looked upon in a number of ways some of which are described below:

(i)   Dardenne et al. [25] state that goals are high-level objectives of the business, organization, or system; they capture the reasons why a system is needed and guide decisions at various levels within the enterprise.

(ii) According to [23], "Goals are targets for achievement which provide a framework for the desired system. Goals are high level objectives of the business, organization, or system."

(iii) According to [13], "Goal is an objective the composite system should meet."

It is also interesting to observe that goals are prescriptive statements as against descriptive statements [26] in that they state what is expected from the system and not statements describing the domain of the system.

Goals have been used in RE for eliciting functional requirements [25] as well as non-functional requirements [11]. Hard goals can be "satisfyced" by the system and used for modeling and analyzing FRs [10]. Satisfaction and information goals are examples of hard goals. Softgoals are goals that do not have a clear-cut criterion for their satisfaction [11] and are used to model and analyze NFRs.

Goals are modeled using the goal decomposition method. It was noticed that goals positively or negatively "support" other goals [27]. These "goal links" are used as the basis for building a refinement tree and the links are expressed in terms of AND/OR associations. Thus, goal models are directed acyclic graphs with the nodes of the graphs representing goals [28] and achievement as edges. An AND association means that all the subgoals, $g1$, ..., gn, must be satisfied to satisfy the parent goal, g. An OR association means that satisfying at least one subgoal, $g1$, ..., gn, is enough to satisfy the parent goal, g. The third link, "conflict", was also added to the refinement tree to capture the case when satisfying one goal caused another goal to not be satisfied. Further links were added to this basic model. van Lamsweerde [13] introduced pre-conditions, post-conditions, and trigger conditions. Link between goals and operations was also introduced by Dardenne et al. [25] where lowest level goals were said to be operational goals. This meant that operational goals can be implemented using functions of a functional system.

Before one can start goal modeling, goals need to be identified. One source of goals is from current systems and documents like ER diagrams, flowcharts, etc. Another source is from stakeholder interviews. Stakeholders own goals, though, requirements, are expressed by them not in terms of goals but as actions and operations [23]. Goals can be extracted from actions by selecting appropriate "action words". It is the agents/actors that fulfill goals. So during goal modeling, goals are identified and then during operationalization, agents are allocated to goals. KAOS method described below though does model agents having wishes and they participate in the RE process.

Two Goal-Oriented Requirements Engineering, GORE, techniques are briefly described below:

- KAOS [25] defines a formal specification language for goal specification consisting of objects, operations, agent, and goal. Objects can be entities, relationships, or events. The elicitation process is in two parts. Initially, an initial set of system goals and objects and an initial set of agents and actions are defined. In the second part, refining goals using AND/OR decomposition, identifying obstacles to goals, operationalizing goals into constraints, and refining and formalizing definitions of objects and actions are done iteratively. Goal refinement ends when every subgoal is realizable by some agent.

- Goal-Based Requirements Analysis Method, GBRAM, Antón [23] identifies, elaborates, and refines the goals as requirements. It deals with two issues. How can goals be identified and what happens to requirements when goals change?

The first part of the question is answered by Goal Analysis and the second part by Goal Evolution. In the former, goals, stakeholders, actors, and constraints are identified. This gives a preliminary set of goals. Once validated by the stake-holders, this initial set can be refined.

It has been observed by Antón and Potts [29] that identifying goals of the system is not the easiest task. GORE is subjective, dependent on the requirements engineer view of the real world from where goals are identified [28]. Horkoff and Yu [30] also point out that such models are "informal and incomplete" and "difficult to precisely define". Horkoff and Yu [31] observe "goal modeling is not yet widely used in practice" [32] and notice that constructs used in KAOS are not used in practice.

1.5.2   Agent-Oriented Requirements Engineering

Agents have been treated in software engineering as autonomous units that can change state and behavior. They can be humans, machine, or any other type. Agents have the following properties [15, 22, 33]:

(i)   Agents are intentional in that they have properties like goals, beliefs, abili-ties, etc. associated with them. These goals are local to the agent. It is important to note that there is no global intention that is captured.
(ii)   Agents have autonomy. However, they can influence and constrain one another. This means that they are related of each other at the intentional level.
(iii)   Agents are in a strategic relationship with each other. They are dependent on each other and are also vulnerable w.r.t. other agents' behavior.

Agents help in defining the rationale and intensions of building the system. This enables them to ask and answer the "why" question. Agent-oriented RE focuses on early RE (see Fig. 1.1).

The central concept is that "goals belong to agents" rather than the concept in GORE where "agents fulfil goals". Notice that even though it is possible to have goals without agents and agents without goals, goals and agents complement each other.

We discuss the i* framework. i* framework was developed for modeling and reasoning the organizational environment and its information system. The central concept of i* is that of the *intentional actor*. This model has two main concepts, the *Strategic Dependency* Model (SDM) and the Strategic *Rationale* Model (SRM). Both early and late phase requirements can be captured through this model.

SDM component of the model describes the actors in their organizational environments and captures the intentional dependencies between them. The free-dom and the constraints of the actors are shown in terms of different dependencies like goal, task, softgoal, and resource dependencies. SRM is at a much lower level of abstraction than SDM. It captures the intentional relationships that are internal and inside actors. Intentional properties are modeled as external dependencies, using means–ends relationships as well as task decomposition. Means–ends relationship helps us understand "why an actor would engage in some task." This can also assist in the discovery of new softgoals and therefore provide more alternate solutions. During modeling, we can travel from means to ends or vice versa. Task decomposition results in hierarchy of intentional elements part of a routine.

Matulevičius and Heymans [32] notice that constructs used in i* are not used in practice. Further, using ontological studies, they found similarities between i* and KAOS. They concluded that constructs like i* goal and soft goal of KAOS, and means–end link of i* and contribution relation of KAOS are conceptually the same.

1.5.3 Scenario Orientation

Scenarios have been used for requirements engineering [34] particularly for elicitation refining and validating requirements, that is, in the late RE phase. Scenarios have also been used to support goals formulated in the early requirements phase. They show whether the system satisfies (fulfillment) or does not satisfy (non-fulfillment) a goal. In other words, scenarios "concretise" goals.

Holbrook [35] states that "Scenarios can be thought of as stories that illustrate how a perceived system will satisfy a user's needs." This indicates that scenarios describe the system from the viewpoint of the user. They have a temporal component as seen in the definition given by van Lamsweerde and Willemet [36]: "a scenario is a temporal sequence of interaction events between the software to-be and its environment in the restricted context of achieving some implicit purpose(s)". Scenarios have also been defined with respect to agents. Plihon et al. [37] say that scenario is "…possible behaviours limited to a subset of purposeful…communications taking place among two or several agents".

A meta schema was proposed by Sutcliffe et al. [34] that shows the relationship between goals, scenarios, and agents. Scenarios are a single instance of a use case. Use cases are composed of actions that help in fulfillment of goals. One use case fulfills one goal. A single action "involves" one or more agents.

Several elicitation techniques exist two of which are described below:

- SBRE [35]: There are two worlds, users' and designers' world. The goal set is defined in the user's world. It contains information regarding goals and constraints of the system. The goals are represented as subgoals. The design set is in the designer's world. This set consists of design models that represent the system. The goal set and the design set communicate with each other with the help of scenarios that is in the scenario set. This set shows how a specific design meets a goal. Scenarios have a one-to-one relationship with the design models. A specific scenario may satisfy many goals. Any issue that may arise is captured in the issue set. A feedback cycle captures the user's response to issue and design. Scenarios form part of the specification of the required system.

- CREWS [34]: This technique is integrated with OO development and employs use cases to model functionality of the system to-be. Here, scenario is represented by one instance of an event which is defined by a pathway of a use case. Thus, many scenarios can be generated from one use case and one scenario is composed of one or more events. Use cases are elicited from users and formatting guidelines. The use cases are compared with generic requirements and finally normal and exception flows are modeled. From the former normal scenarios and from the latter exception, scenarios are generated. They are validated using validation frames. Scenarios originated from system design and those captured from actual experience are captured by this technique.

1.5.4 Goal–Scenario Coupling

Proposals for goal–scenario coupling also exist in literature [38–41]. This can be unidirectional from goals to scenarios or bidirectional coupling of goals and scenarios. Unidirectional coupling says that goals are realized by scenarios and this reveals how goals can be achieved. Bidirectional coupling considers going from scenario to goals in addition to going from goals to scenarios. It says that scenarios can be sources of subgoals of the goal for which the scenario is written.

1.6 Conclusion

Origins of Requirements and Requirements Engineering, RE, lie in Information Systems/Software Engineering (SE) with the aim to deliver the needed functionality in the hands of the user. The system development task starts when requirements are elicited from users, collected, and prioritized, and a system specification is made.

The area of agile development has grown independently of the subject of requirements engineering. Therefore, the influence of one on the other has been rather limited.

In the next chapter, we will consider the impact of transactional requirements engineering on data warehouse requirements engineering. We will also see that given the complexity of data warehouse systems, agility is of the essence. Therefore, the influence of agile development on data warehouse development shall also be taken up in the next chapter.

References

1. Chaos Report, Standish Group. (1994).
2. Hooks, I. F., & Farry, K. A. (2001). *Customer-centered products: Creating successful products through smart requirements management.* New York: AMACOM Div American Mgmt Assn.
3. Boehm, B. W., & Papaccio, P. N. (1988). Understanding and controlling software costs. *IEEE Transactions on Software Engineering, 14*(10), 1462–1477.
4. Standish Group. (2003). *Chaos Chronicles Version 3.0.* West Yarmouth, MA.
5. Charette, R. N. (2005). Why software FAILS. *IEEE Spectrum, 42*(9), 42–49.
6. Wake, W. C. (2003). *INVEST in good stories and SMART tasks.* Retrieved December 29, 2005. From http://xp123.com/xplor/xp0308/index.shtml.
7. IEEE Standard, IEEE-Std 610. (1990).
8. Robertson, S., & Robertson, J. (2012). *Mastering the requirements process: Getting requirements right.* MA: Addison-wesley.
9. Kotonya, G., & Sommerville, I. (1998). *Requirements engineering: Processes and techniques.* New York: Wiley.
10. Sutcliffe, A. (2002). *User-centred requirements engineering.* Berlin: Springer.
11. Mylopoulos, J., Chung, L., & Yu, E. (1999). From object-oriented to goal-oriented requirements analysis. *Communications of the ACM, 42*(1), 31–37.
12. Zave, P. (1997). Classification of research efforts in requirements engineering. *ACM Computing Surveys (CSUR), 29*(4), 315–321.
13. van Lamsweerde, A. (2000, June). Requirements engineering in the year 00: A research perspective. In *Proceedings of the 22nd International Conference on Software Engineering* (pp. 5–19). New York: ACM.
14. Nuseibeh, B., & Easterbrook, S. (2000, May). Requirements engineering: A roadmap. In *Proceedings of the Conference on the Future of Software Engineering* (pp. 35–46). New York: ACM.
15. Yu, E. S. (1997, January). Towards modelling and reasoning support for early-phase requirements engineering. In *Proceedings of the Third IEEE International Symposium on Requirements Engineering* (pp. 226–235). IEEE.
16. Goguen, J. A., & Linde, C. (1993). Techniques for requirements elicitation. *Requirements Engineering, 93,* 152–164.
17. Suchman, L., & Jordan, B. (1990). Interactional troubles in face-to-face survey interviews. *Journal of the American Statistical Association, 85*(409), 232–241.
18. Hickey, A., & Davis, A. (2003). Barriers to transferring requirements elicitation techniques to practice. In *2003 Business Information Systems Conference.*
19. Leffingwell, D., & Widrig, D. (2000). *Managing software requirements.* MA: Addison-Wesley.
20. Davis, G. B. (1982). Strategies for information requirements determination. *IBM Systems Journal, 21,* 4–30.
21. Burton, A. M., Shadbolt, N. R., Rugg, G., & Hedgecock, A. P. (1990). The efficacy of knowledge elicitation techniques: A comparison across domains and levels of expertise. *Journal of Knowledge Acquisition, 2,* 167–178.
22. Lapouchnian, A. (2005). Goal-oriented requirements engineering: An overview of the current research. University of Toronto.
23. Antón, A. I. (1996, April). Goal-based requirements analysis. In *Proceedings of the Second International Conference on Requirements Engineering* (pp. 136–144). IEEE.
24. van Lamsweerde, A. (2004, September). Goal-oriented requirements engineering: A roundtrip from research to practice engineering. In *Requirements Engineering Conference, 2004. Proceedings. 12th IEEE International* (pp. 4–7). IEEE.
25. Dardenne, A., van Lamsweerde, A., & Fickas, S. (1993). Goal-directed requirements acquisition. *Science of Computer Programming, 20*(1), 3–50.

26. Pohl, K. (2010). *Requirements engineering: Fundamentals, principles, and techniques.* Berlin: Springer.
27. van Lamsweerde, A. (2001). Goal-oriented requirements engineering: A guided tour. In *Proceedings. Fifth IEEE International Symposium on Requirements Engineering, 2001* (pp. 249–262). IEEE.
28. Haumer, P., Pohl, K., & Weidenhaupt, K. (1998). Requirements elicitation and validation with real world scenes. *IEEE Transactions on, Software Engineering, 24*(12), 1036–1054.
29. Antón, A. I., & Potts, C. (1998, April). The use of goals to surface requirements for evolving systems. In *Proceedings of the 1998 International Conference on Software Engineering, 1998* (pp. 157–166). IEEE.
30. Horkoff, J., & Yu, E. (2010). Interactive analysis of agent-goal models in enterprise modeling. *International Journal of Information System Modeling and Design (IJISMD), 1*(4), 1–23.
31. Horkoff, J., & Yu, E. (2012). Comparison and evaluation of goal-oriented satisfaction analysis techniques. *Requirement Engineering Journal,* 1–24.
32. Matulevičius, R., & Heymans, P. (2007). Comparing goal modelling languages: An experiment. *Requirements engineering: Foundation for software quality* (pp. 18–32). Berlin Heidelberg: Springer.
33. Castro, J., Kolp, M., & Mylopoulos, J. (2002). Towards requirements-driven information systems engineering: The Tropos project. *Information Systems, 27*(6), 365–389.
34. Sutcliffe, A. G., Maiden, N. A., Minocha, S., & Manuel, D. (1998). Supporting scenario-based requirements engineering. *IEEE Transactions on Software Engineering, 24* (12), 1072–1088.
35. Holbrook, H., III. (1990). A scenario-based methodology for conducting requirements elicitation. *ACM SIGSOFT Software Engineering Notes, 15*(1), 95–104.
36. van Lamsweerde, A., & Willemet, L. (1998). Inferring declarative requirements specifications from operational scenarios. *IEEE Transactions on Software Engineering, 24*(12), 1089–1114.
37. Plihon, V., Ralyte, J., Benjamen, A., Maiden, N. A., Sutcliffe, A., Dubois, E., & Heymans, P. (1998). A reuse-oriented approach for the construction of scenario bases methods. In *Proceedings of International Conference on Software Process* (pp. 1–16).
38. Liu, L., & Yu, E. (2004). Designing information systems in social context: A goal and scenario modelling approach. *Information Systems, 29*(2), 187–203.
39. CREWS Team. (1998). The CREWS glossary, CREWS report 98-1. http://SUNSITE. informatik.rwth-aachen.de/CREWS/reports.htm.
40. Pohl, K., & Haumer, P. (1997, June). Modelling contextual information about scenarios. In *Proceedings of the Third International Workshop on Requirements Engineering: Foundations of Software Quality REFSQ* (Vol. 97, pp. 187–204).
41. Cockburn, A. (1997). Structuring use cases with goals, 1997. *Journal of Object-Oriented Programming.*

Chapter 2
Requirements Engineering for Data Warehousing

Whereas in the last chapter we considered transactional systems, in this chapter we consider data warehouse systems. The former kind of systems deals with delivering system functionality in the hands of the user. However, the latter does not carry out any action. Rather such systems supply information to their users who are decision-makers, so that they could take appropriate decisions. These decisions are made after decision-makers carry out suitable analysis of the information retrieved from the data warehouse.

In this chapter, we consider the manner in which data warehouses are developed. In Sect. 2.1, we provide a brief background of data warehousing so as to form the basis for the rest of the chapter. In Sect. 2.2, we look at some studies that bring out the problems experienced in developing data warehouses. The Systems Development Life Cycle, SDLC for Data warehouses, DWSDLC, is the subject of Sect. 2.3. The methods that can be used to realize this life cycle are presented in Sect. 2.4. These methods are the monolithic, top-down approach, data mart approach, and the agile approach. The problem of consolidation that arises in the data mart and agile approaches is considered thereafter in Sect. 2.5.

Success of a data warehouse project is crucially dependent on its alignment with the business environment in which it is to function. It is important therefore to involve business people in planning and laying out a roadmap for data warehouse roll-out. We identify, in Sect. 2.6, the several factors that go into making good alignment and highlight the role of requirements engineering. Thereafter, in Sect. 2.7 we present a survey of data warehouse requirements engineering techniques.

2.1 Data Warehouse Background

There are two perspectives to data warehousing, the organizational and the technological. From the organizational standpoint, data warehouse technology is for providing service to the organization: it provides Business Intelligence, BI. The

© Springer Nature Singapore Pte Ltd. 2018
N. Prakash and D. Prakash, *Data Warehouse Requirements Engineering*,
https://doi.org/10.1007/978-981-10-7019-8_2

Data Warehouse Institute considers BI in three parts, namely, data warehousing, tools for business analytics, and knowledge management. The value of BI [1] is realized as profitable business action. This means that BI is of little value if knowledge that can be used for profitable action is ignored. Conversely, if discovered knowledge is not realized into a value-producing action, then it is of little value. Thus, managers should be able to obtain **the specific information** that helps in making **the optimal decision** so that **specific actions can be taken**. It follows that Business Intelligence [1] incorporates the tools, methods, and processes needed to transform data into actionable knowledge.

Turning now to the technological point of view, the classical definition of a data warehouse was provided by Inmon, according to which a data warehouse is a "subject-oriented, integrated, time variant, non-volatile collection of data" for supporting management's decisional needs. Another view is to look upon a "data warehouse as the data, processes, tools, and facilities to manage and deliver complete, timely, accurate, and understandable business information to authorized individuals for effective decision-making". According to this view, a data warehouse is not just a storehouse of data but is an environment or infrastructure for decision-making.

The central difference between a data warehouse and a database lies in what they aim to deliver. The former supports Online Analytical Processing, OLAP, whereas the latter is for Online Transaction Processing, OLTP. A database contains in it data of all transactions that were performed during business operations. Thus, for example, data of every order received is available in the database. If modification of the order occurred, then the modified data is available. In this sense, a database is an image, a snapshot of the state of the business at a given moment, T. Though it is possible that data in databases is specifically timestamped to keep historical data, normally databases do not maintain historical data but reflect data at current time T only.

In contrast, the purpose of the data warehouse is to provide information to facilitate making a business decision. Interest is in analyzing the state of the business at time t (this may include current data at t as well as historical data) so as to determine what went wrong and needs correction, what to promote, what to optimize and, in general, to decide how to make the business perform better. The state of the business lies in the collection of data sources of the business, the several databases, files, spreadsheets, documents, emails, etc. at time t. Therefore, a data warehouse at t is a collection of all this information. Unlike a database that is updated each time a new transaction occurs, a data warehouse is refreshed at well-defined refresh times. Thus, the data warehouse does not necessarily contain the current state of the business, that is, t may be older than current time t'. In other words, it is possible that data in the data warehouse may be older than that currently contained in the individual data sources of the business. For purposes of decision-making, this is tolerable so long as business events between t and t' do not make decisions based on data at t irrelevant.

This difference between a database and a data warehouse makes the usual create, update, and delete operations of a database largely irrelevant to a data warehouse. The traditional relational read is also found to be very restrictive, and a more versatile way of querying the data warehouse is needed. In other words, we need a different model of data than the database model. This OLAP model enables data to be viewed and operated upon to promote analysis of business data.

A data warehouse provides a multidimensional view of data. Data is viewed in terms of facts and dimensions, a fact being the basic data that is to be analyzed, whereas dimensions are the various parameters along which facts are analyzed. Both facts and dimensions have their own attributes. Thus, sales data expressed as number of units sold or in revenue terms (rupees, dollars) is basic sales data that can be analyzed by location, customer profile, and time. These latter are the dimensions.

The n-dimensions provide an n-dimensional space in which facts are placed. A three-dimensional fact is thus represented as a cube (see Fig. 2.1). The X-, Y-, and Z-axes of the cube represent the three dimensions, and the cells of the cube contain facts. For our example, the three axes correspond to location, customer profile, and time, respectively. Each cell in the cube contains sales data, i.e., units sold or revenue. Of course facts may have more than three dimensions. These form hypercubes but often in data warehouse terminology, the words cubes and hyper-cubes are used interchangeably.

It is possible for attributes of dimensions to be organized in a hierarchy. For example, the attributes month, quarter, half year, and year of the dimension time form a hierarchy. Monthly facts can be aggregated into quarterly, half-yearly, and yearly facts, respectively. Such aggregations may be computed "on the fly" or, once computed, may be physically materialized. In the reverse direction, one can obtain finer grained information by moving from yearly facts to half-yearly, quarterly, and monthly facts, respectively.

The multidimensional structure comes with its own operations for Online Analytical Processing, OLAP. These operations are as follows:

Fig. 2.1 A three-dimensional fact

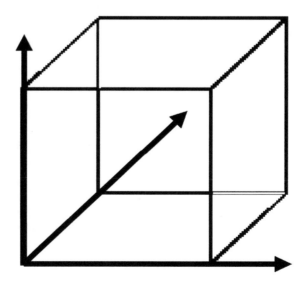

- Roll up: aggregating by moving up the hierarchy as described above.
- Drill down: inverse of roll up. As described above, this operation is for obtaining finer data from aggregated/rolled up data.
- Pivot or Rotate: in order to visualize the faces of a cube, the cube is rotated in space.
- Slice: generates a cube that has one fewer dimension than the original cube. So, for one dimension, a single value is chosen thus creating a rectangular, two-dimensional, subset of the original cube.
- Dice: here, specific values across multiple dimensions are picked yielding a sub-cube.
- Drill across: this operation allows obtaining data from two different cubes that have common (conformed) dimensions.

Designers of multidimensional structures need knowledge of the information that is of interest in the organization. This information is then converted into facts and dimensions that are expressed in the model adopted by the data warehouse package (Cognos, SQL server, Hyperion, etc.) used for implementation. Finally, the physical structure of the data warehouse, the partitions, etc. needs to be defined. Broadly, we have three steps, conceptual design for developing a conceptual schema of the needed information, logical design for obtaining and representing facts and dimensions, and physical design for defining the physical properties of the data warehouse. These three phases are similar to the corresponding phases in databases: conceptual design refers to a semantic abstraction that results in, for example, entity relationship schema of the database, logical design refers to representation as relations, and physical design to the indices, buffers, etc. required for an optimal physical layout of the database.

A major difference between data warehouse development and database development is due to the need in the former to draw data from disparate data sources. This is done in the Extraction Transformation and Loading, ETL, step where data is taken from the different sources, standardized, any inconsistencies removed, and thereafter the data is brought into multidimensional form. This "cleaned up" data is then loaded in the data warehouse. Though data preparation, entry, and initially populating the data are important in databases, it is nowhere near as complex as the ETL process is. As we will see, the presence of the ETL step has an important bearing on data warehouse project management.

2.2 Data Warehouse Development Experience

Data warehouses have been developed for the last 25 years or so. The broad learning is that data warehouse projects are complex, time-consuming, and expensive. They are also risky and have a high propensity to fail. Often, they do not meet expectations and have a poor record of delivering the promised products. As a result, there are issues concerning data warehouse project management as well as around DWSDLC.

A number of studies have found that data warehouse projects are expensive in financial terms as well as in terms of the effort required to deliver them. In [2], we find a number of specific indicators:

- One company hired the services of a well-qualified systems integrator. It cost two million USD and after 3 years time they got a single report but not a working system.
- Having bought a ready to use data model, another company found that it needed 2 years to customize the model to their needs and 3 years to populate it with their data. Only after that would they get their first outputs.
- Yet another company required 150 people for over 3 years and the project got so expensive as to hurt their share price.

Aside from being expensive, data warehouse projects are risky. Ericson [3] cites a survey showing that data warehouse projects whose cost averaged above $12M failed 65% of the time. Hayen et al. [4] refer to studies that indicate the typical cost of a data warehouse project to be one million dollars in the very first year and that one-half to two-thirds of most data warehouse projects fail.

Loshin [1] points out that data warehouse projects generate high expectations but bring many disappointments. This is due to failure in the way that DW projects are taken from conception through to implementation. This is corroborated by [2] who concludes that the lessons learnt from data warehouse projects covered the entire development life cycle:

- **Requirements**: The business had little idea of what they wanted because they had never experienced a data warehouse. Further, requirements gathering should have been done better.
- **Design**: Design took a very long time and conflicting definitions of data made designs worthless.
- **Coding**: It went slow, testing came under pressure, and crucial defects were not caught.

The implications of the foregoing were deviations from initial cost estimates, reduced number and value of the delivered features, and long delivery time.

The conclusion of Alshboul [5] is that one of the causes of data warehouse project failure is inadequate determination of the relationship of the DW with strategic business requirements.

From the foregoing, we observe in Table 2.1 that there are three main causes of data warehouse project failure. The first is inadequate DW-business alignment. It is necessary to ensure that the data warehouse brings "value" to the organization. This is possible if the data warehouse delivers information relevant to making business decisions.

The second issue is that of requirements gathering. In its early years, data warehouse requirements engineering was de-emphasized. Indeed, requirements were the last thing to be discovered [6]. However, considerable effort has been put in the last 15 years or so to systematize requirements engineering. Starting from

Table 2.1 Failure and its mitigation strategies

Failure cause	Mitigating failure
Inadequate alignment of DW with business needs	Relate information to business decisional needs
Requirements gathering	Systematize and broad base the requirements gathering process
Project delivery	Reduce long delivery time

initial, ad hoc techniques we have seen the emergence of model-driven requirements engineering.

Finally, we have the issue of project delivery and long delivery times. We need to move beyond the waterfall model. Stage-wise delivery does not allow a downstream DWSDLC activity to be completed till upstream activities of the development life cycle are completed. In large development warehouse projects, this leads to unacceptable delays in product delivery. We need a development method that produces a steady stream of product deliverables as early as possible from the time the project starts.

2.3 Data Warehouse Systems Development Life Cycle, DWSDLC

The activities that are to be performed in order to develop a data warehouse are laid out in the DWSDLC. The manner in which these activities are performed is defined in process models. For example, in the waterfall model, the activities comprising the SDLC are performed in a linear manner: an activity is performed when the previous one is completed. It is possible to do development in an iterative and incremental manner in which case this strict linear ordering is not followed.

It is interesting to see the evolution of DWSDLC over the years. In its early years, data warehouse development was largely concerned with implementation issues. Therefore, upstream activities of conceptual design and requirements engineering were de-emphasized. Data warehouse development started from analysis of data in existing databases. The nature of this analysis was largely experience based and data warehouse developers used their expertise to determine the needed facts and dimensions. This was viewed in [7], in terms of the requirements, conceptual design, and construction stages of the DWSDLC. In the requirements stage, facts and preliminary workload information are obtained starting from a database schema. Subsequently, in conceptual design, the database schema, workload, and facts are all used to obtain the dimensional schema.

Notice that there is no real conceptualization of the data warehouse as no conceptual schema is built. The process of identifying dimensions is not apparent and seems to rely on designer insight and understanding of information requirements of the decision-maker. The nature of the requirements engineering activity is also rather ad hoc. Thus, the manner in which facts and workload are obtained, the underlying modeling and systematization of this process, is not articulated. Little effort is made to go beyond existing database schema and no real enquiry to identify any other needed information is launched. Finally, there is no assurance that the resulting data warehouse does, indeed, address decision-making needs. This is because not much effort is put into interacting with decision-makers to determine their information needs.

Conceptual Design Stage

The next step in SDLC evolution was the introduction of a conceptual design stage. The argument was that conceptual schemas like the ER schema could be good starting points since they captured the entire information to be kept in the data warehouse. This could then be analyzed together with domain experts to determine interesting measures, dimensions, and initial OLAP queries. Thereafter, a multi-dimensional schema is built that is taken into the construction phase.

The approach of Hüsemann et al. [8] produces measures and dimensional attributes of the data warehouse from ER schemas of databases. The E/R schema is assumed to be available to the data warehouse designer. If not, then it can either be reverse engineered by using various tools/algorithms or built afresh. The domain expert picks up the relevant operational attributes needed for multidimensional analysis and specifies the purpose of using them in a tabular form. The tabulation of the dimensional attributes obtained is then converted into a dimensional schema. This schema in a graphical form comprises fact schemas along with their dimension hierarchies and fact attributes or measures.

There are two main drawbacks with this technique. First, there is no defined method that helps the designer in identifying the facts, dimensions, and measures. Similarly, determining aggregates requires designers to be experienced and skilled. The absence of guidance in these tasks means that the process is essentially an art.

The second method [9] based on the ER diagram also derives data warehouse structures from ER schemas. As before, if an ER schema does not exist, then either it is to be developed or reverse engineered from existing databases. The proposal is that entities are classified as transaction entities, component entities, or classification entities. Transaction entities form fact tables. Component entities and classification entities form dimension tables and answer the "who", "what", "when", "where", "how", and "why" of business events. All hierarchies that exist in the data model are identified. In the final stage, dimensional models are produced from the identified entities.

This second method also offers no guidance in selecting which transaction entities are important for decision-making and therefore become facts. A precedence hierarchy for resolving ambiguities that arise during classifying entities has been defined. But again no guidance in terms of an algorithm or method has been provided.

Golfarelli et al. [10] developed a process that can be used for converting an ER diagram into multidimensional form. This is partially automated and requires developers to bring additional knowledge to decide on the final multidimensional structure.

Moving to the conceptual design stage did present one major advantage over database schema-based approaches. This move was based on the argument that the process of discovery of data warehouse concepts should be rooted in an analysis of the conceptual schema. Thus, it provided a foundation for obtaining facts, dimensions, etc. It contributed to somewhat de-mystifying this process.

Conceptual schema/ER-driven techniques have been criticized on several grounds:

- Limited data: If reverse engineered from operational databases, then the information carried by ER schemas is limited to that in the database schema. It is difficult to identify sources that are both external and other internal sources [7].
- Modeling deficiencies: ER schemas are not designed to model historical information as well as aggregate information, both of which are so important in data warehousing.
- Ignoring the user: ER-based techniques do not give primary importance to the users' perspective [10, 11]. As a result, the DW designer ends up deciding on the relevance of data but this decision should be taken by the user and not by designers.

The Requirements Engineering Stage

The introduction of the requirements engineering stage in the DWSDLC addressed the concerns raised in conceptual schema-driven techniques. A clear effort was made to take into account needs of stakeholders in the data warehouse to-be. The definition of multidimensional structures was based on understanding of business goals, business services, and business processes. This understanding was gained by interaction with decision-makers. Thus, the context of the data warehouse was explored and the requirements of the data warehouse to-be were seen to originate in the business. Since ab initio investigation into decision-maker needs is carried out in the requirements engineering stage, existing data sources and/or their conceptualization in conceptual schemas did not impose any limitations. Rather, the determined requirements could use data from existing data sources or come up with completely new data not available in these sources.

With the introduction of the requirements engineering stage in DWSDLC, there is today no difference between the stages of the TSDLC of transactional systems and stages of the DWSDLC. However, the tasks carried out in these stages are different. This is brought out in Table 2.2.

It is important to notice that the problem of data warehouse requirements engineering, DWRE, is that of determining the information that shall be contained in the data warehouse to-be. On the other hand, requirements engineering for transactional systems, TRE, aims to identify the needed functionality of the

Table 2.2 SDLCs of transactional and data warehouse systems

SDLC stage	Transactional systems	Data warehouse systems
Requirements engineering	Defining system functionality	Defining needed information
Conceptual design	Building the conceptual schema: structural, behavioral, functional models	Building structural schema
Construction	Implementing the functions	Implementing the multidimensional structure

transactional system to-be. This functionality is eventually to be implemented in the construction stage of the TSDLC, for which a suitable design must be produced in the conceptual design stage. This design is expressed in structural, behavioral, and functional models and typically expressed in UML notation. In contrast, in the construction stage of the DWSDLC, the determined information must be collected from disparate sources, standardized and made consistent, and integrated together to populate the multidimensional schema. For this, a multidimensional structure must be obtained. It is traditional to focus on this structural aspect, and consequently, expression in behavioral and functional models is de-emphasized.

There are two ways in which the DWSDLC supports determination of multidimensional structures. The first is (see Fig. 2.2a) to consider the requirements engineering stage as not only producing the required information but also the facts and dimensions. In this way, there is no need for the conceptual schema in the form of an ER schema to be built. Instead, a direct translation to facts/dimensions is done. The second way (shown in Fig. 2.2b) is to build the conceptual schema and then use any of the methods for obtaining facts/dimensions proposed in ER-driven approach outlined earlier. We will see requirements engineering techniques of these two kinds in the next section. The possibility of skipping over the conceptual design stage is a major variation between TSDLC and DWSDLC.

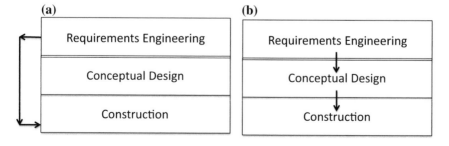

Fig. 2.2 **a** Bypassing conceptual stage, **b** using all stages

2.4 Methods for Data Warehouse Development

Methods for developing data warehouses need to go through the stages of the DWSDLC. There are two possibilities, to traverse the DWSDLC breadth first or depth first. The breadth-first approach calls for the three stages in the DWSDLC to be done sequentially, construction after conceptual design after requirements engineering. The depth-first approach breaks down the task of data warehouse development into small pieces or vertical slices, and the DWSDLC is followed for each slice produced.

2.4.1 Monolithic Versus Bus Architecture

Breadth-first traversal can be done based on two different assumptions. The first assumption is that the deliverable is the complete data warehouse. Hence, requirements of the entire data warehouse must be identified; the multidimensional model for the enterprise must be designed and then taken into implementation. Thereafter, specific subject-oriented data marts are defined so as to make appropriate subsets of the data warehouse available to specific users. This is shown in Fig. 2.3 where sales, purchase, and production data marts are built on top of the enterprise-wide data warehouse. Defining data marts in this manner is analogous to construction of subschemas on the schema of a database. The main idea in both is to provide a limited view of the totality, limited to that which is relevant to specific users.

This approach of constructing the monolithic data warehouse follows the waterfall model; each stage of the DWSDLC must be completed before moving to the next stage. This implies that lead time in delivering the project is very high. There is danger that the requirements might change even as work is in progress. In

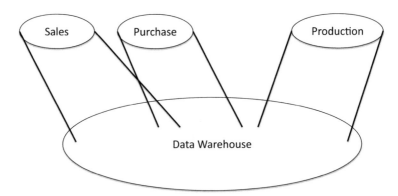

Fig. 2.3 Monolithic development

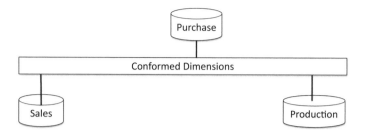

Fig. 2.4 The bus architecture

short, monolithic development is prone to all problems associated with the waterfall model of development. However, the likely benefit from the waterfall model is that it could produce a long-lasting and reliable data architecture.

A different process model results if the assumption of delivering the full data warehouse is relaxed. Rather than building the entire monolithic data warehouse, this approach calls for first building data marts and then integrating them by putting them on a common bus. This bus consists of conformed dimensions, dimensions that are common across data marts, and therefore allow the drill across operation to be performed. Consequently, data held in different data marts can be retrieved. This approach is shown in Fig. 2.4.

Data marts are built independently of one another. Since the size of a data mart is smaller than the entire data warehouse, the lead time for release is lesser. Therefore, business value can be provided even with the release of the first data mart. Freshly built data marts can then be added on to the bus. Thus, the data warehouse consists of a number of integrated, self-contained data marts rather than a big centralized data warehouse. Evidently, the bus approach promotes iterative and incremental development and no complete plan is required upfront. The risks are that data marts may contain missing or incompatible measures and dimensions contain replicated data and display inconsistent results.

The success of the bus architecture is crucially dependent on conforming facts and dimensions. Thus, if one data mart contains product information in number of cases shipped and another keeps product information as units sold, then moving across these data marts yields incompatible information. Such facts must be conformed, by keeping, along with shipping data, unit data as well. This allows units shipped to be compared with units sold. Dimensions need to be conformed too. If one data mart has attributes day, quarter, and year for the dimension time and another has day and month half year, then drill across becomes difficult. The dimension attributes must be made to conform and the lowest granularity attribute kept in both the dimensions. The product information must also be available on a daily basis in our example.

There are two possibilities for conforming dimensions. The first is to do it "on the fly", as each new data mart is added on to the bus. This may involve reworking existing data marts to make them conform. This can be adopted so long as the effort to bring about conformity is within limits and does not offset the benefits involved in doing early release. When this boundary is crossed, then attention must be paid to designing for conformity. This means that the bus of conformed dimensions must be determined either all upfront in the waterfall model style or enough investigation should be carried out to get a modicum of assurance that the bus is well defined. The trade-off between the two is apparent, delayed release versus the risk of rework.

2.4.2   Data Warehouse Agile Methods

Iterative and incremental development that forms the basis for the bus architecture is at the core of agile methods. Indeed, agility has been extended to data warehouse development as well. However, agile methods for data warehousing, which we refer to as DW-agile methods, differ from agile methods for transactional systems or T-agile methods. We bring these out by considering two DW-agile methods.

Using Scrum and User Stories

In Hughes [2], we see the adoption in DW-agile methods of notions of sprint and user stories of T-agile methods. Recall that user stories are not complete requirements specifications but identify the needs with the details left to be discovered as the sprint progresses. Defining user stories is an "art" and defining good stories requires experienced story writers. Story writing follows the epic–theme–story trajectory and the INVEST test is applied to test if a story is appropriately defined or not. Over several decades, in order for teams to better author user stories, agile practitioners have devised a number of strategies and tools. Since a user story aims to answer the "who," "what," and "why" of a product; a more detailed examination of these components is suggested. Strategies like user role modeling, vision boxes, and product boards have also been devised. Finally, Hughes also introduced the T-agile roles of product owner, Scrum master, and the development team in DW-agile methods.

The point of real departure in DW-agile methods is reached when defining sprints for doing data integration. During this stage, data from disparate sources is brought together in a (a) staging area, (b) integrated, (c) converted into dimensional form, and (d) dashboards are built. This is to be done for each fact and dimension comprising the multidimensional schema. Thus, we get four sprints, one each for (a) to (d): one sprint that does (a) for all facts and dimensions of the schema, another that does (b), and so on, for all the four stages. If we now ask the question, what is the value delivered by each sprint and to whom, then we do not get a straightforward answer. Indeed, no business value is delivered at the end of sprints for (a) to (c) to any stakeholder. The only role aware that progress in the task of delivering the data warehouse is being made is the product owner but this role is not the end user.

The Data Warehouse Business Intelligence, DWBI, reference data architecture shown in Fig. 2.5 makes the foregoing clearer. This architecture separates DWBI data and processes into two layers, back end and front end. Within the back end part, we have sub-layers for staging, integration, and presentation sub-part relevant to integration, whereas the front end layer comprises the presentation sub-layer interfaces to the sematic sub-layer, the semantic sub-layer as well as the dashboard sub-layer.

Delivering a dashboard requires the preceding four layers to be delivered and can be likened to delivery of four applications rolled into one. Delivering such a large application is unlikely to be done in a single sprint of a few weeks in duration and needs to be broken down into sub-deliverables.

To deal with this, Hughes introduces the idea of developer stories. A developer story is linked to a user story and is expressed in a single sentence in the who–what–why form of user stories. However, these stories have the product owner as the end user and are defined by the development team. A developer story provides value to the product owner and is a step in delivering business value to the stakeholder. It defines a sprint. Developer stories must pass the DILBERT'S test;

Fig. 2.5 The DWBI reference data architecture

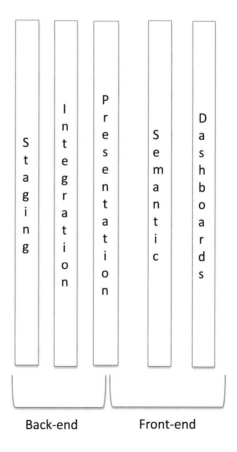

they should be demonstrable, independent, layered, business valued, estimable, refinable, testable, and small. Large developer stories are made smaller by decomposing them.

The difference between user stories and developer stories lies in the Demonstrable, D, and Layered, L, elements of the DILBERT'S test. The other elements of DILBERT'S test can be mapped to elements of the INVEST test for user stories. Let us consider the meanings of these two as follows:

1. Demonstrable indicates that at the end of a sprint for the developer story, the development team should demonstrate the result achieved to the product owner. There are several benefits of this demonstration. For example, involvement of the product owner could enable a check on the quality of the data in source systems and an assessment of whether the staged data is adequate for business decision-making. Similarly, transformations and dashboards could be checked out.

   Equally importantly, Demonstrability provides assurance to the product owner that the development team is making progress. If required, the product owner could even obtain some operations relevant to the business to convince end users about this progress and also obtain feedback.

2. Layered: Each developer story must show progress in only one layer of the DWBI reference data architecture. This promotes independence of developer stories (the I in DILBERT'S).

Introduction of developer stories requires a number of additional roles, other than the three roles of product owner, Scrum master, and development team. These are as follows:

- Project architect: This role is for conceptualizing the application and communicating it to both business stakeholders as well as to technical people. The job involves relating source data to target data in a presentation layer and formulating the major functions of the dashboards.
- Data architect ensures that the semantics of the data are clear, manages the data models of the various layers, implements normalization, etc.
- Systems analyst: Starting from user stories, determines the transformations of source data required to meet business needs. In doing so, the systems analyst will need to look at developer stories to determine the transformations across the multiple layers of the DWBI reference architecture. This role may also need to work with the data architect to define any integrity constraints that must be satisfied by the data before it is accepted into the next layer.
- Systems tester: To ascertain if the build is correct and complete. This is done on a daily basis, at the end of each iteration and when a release is issued. It is normally done at the end of each day.

In the DW-agile method considered above, the issue of how the conformed bus is built is not addressed. Presumably, it is to be built "on the fly" since no provision has been made in the method to build the bus.

Using Agile Data Modeling: Data Stories

Yet, another approach to developing data warehouses in an agile manner is that of Business Event Analysis and Modeling, BEAM* [12]. This method is based on Agile Data Modeling. The argument behind using Agile Data Modeling is that techniques like Scrum and user stories will improve BI *application development* but only once the data warehouse is already in position. However, not much guidance is available in such techniques for developing the *data warehouse* per se. Therefore, we must move towards building the dimensional models in an agile manner. This is where the role of Agile Data Modeling lies.

Agile Data Modeling [13] is for exploring data-oriented structures. It provides for incremental, iterative, and collaborative data modeling. **Incremental data modeling** refers to availability of more requirements when they are better understood or become clear to the stakeholder. The additional requirements are obtained "on the fly" when the developer needs them for completing the implementation task at hand. **Iterative data modeling** emphasizes reworking to improve existing work. As requirements become better understood and as need for changing data schemas is felt, correcting errors, including missing information just discovered and other such rework, referred to as refactoring in the data warehouse community, is carried out. **Collaborative data modeling** calls for close interaction between the developers and stakeholders in obtaining and modeling data requirements. Thus, it moves away from merely eliciting and documenting data requirements with stakeholder participation but also includes stakeholder participation in modeling of data.

BEAM* uses the notion of data stories that are told by stakeholders to capture data about business events that comprise business processes. These data stories are answers to seven types of questions about events and each answer provides a fact or dimension of the multidimensional schema. These questions, called 7W, are (1) Who is involved in the event? (2) What did they do? To what is it done? (3) When did it happen? (4) Where did it take place? (5) Why did it happen? (6) How did it happen—in what manner? (7) How many or much was recorded— how can it be measured? Out of these, the first six supply dimensions whereas the last one supplies facts. As an example, the event, order delivered, can have three "who"-type dimensions, namely, Customer, Product, Carrier and two "when"-type dimensions, order date and shipment date.

Even as facts and dimensions are being discovered, stakeholder–developer interaction attempts to make them conform. The key issue is ensuring that identification of conformed facts and dimensions is done in an agile manner. To do this an event matrix is built. This matrix has business events as rows and dimensions as columns. There is a special column in the matrix, labeled as Importance that contains a number to show the importance of the event. Associated with each row is

Table 2.3 The event matrix

	Importance	Dimension$_1$	Dimension$_2$	Dimension$_i$	Dimension$_n$
Importance		610	640	650	430
Event$_1$	700				
Event$_2$	600				
Event$_j$	500				
Event$_m$	200				

an indication of the importance of the event of the row and similarly a row labeled Importance contains the importance of the dimension (Table 2.3).

When associating dimensions with events, the product owner initiates discussions to make sure that there is agreement on the meaning of dimensions across the different events to which these are applicable. As a result, conformed dimensions are entered into the event matrix.

It is possible to follow the waterfall model and build the event matrix for all events in all processes in the organization. However, agility is obtained when just enough events have been identified so as to enable defining the next sprint. Further, a prioritization of the backlog on the basis of the Importance value is done. Thus, the event matrix is the backlog.

Events have event stories associated with them. Since conformed dimensions have already been identified, it is expected that event stories will be written using these. The expression of events is as a table whose attributes are (a) specific to the event and (b) are the conformed dimensions already obtained from the event matrix. The table is filled in with event stories; each event story is a row of the event table. An event table is filled in with several event stories so as to ensure that all stakeholders agree on the meaning of each attribute in the event table. If there is no agreement, then attributes that are homonyms have been discovered and separate attributes for each meaning must be defined.

Reports that are desired by stakeholders are captured in report stories. These stories are taken further to do data profiling and then on to development in a sprint. This is the BI *application* aspect of data warehouse development.

2.5 Data Mart Consolidation

As seen in the previous section, there are essentially two kinds of data marts as follows:

- Dependent data marts: These are built from an already operational data warehouse and so data for the data mart is extracted directly from the latter. Therefore, such data marts have data which has already been integrated as part of developing the data warehouse. Data in a dependent data mart will also, quite naturally, be consistent with the data in the enterprise data warehouse. The enterprise data warehouse represents the "single version of the truth" and these data marts comply with this.

- Independent data marts: Developed independently from the enterprise data warehouse, these are populated with data often directly from an application, an OLTP database or operational data sources. Consequently, data is not integrated and is likely to be inconsistent with the data warehouse. Independent data marts are built by several different teams using technologies preferred by these teams. Therefore, there is a proliferation of tools, software, hardware, and processes. Clearly, the foregoing happens if conformity across data marts is handled on the fly. Notice, however, that this happens even if consolidation is designed for as in BEAM* because post-design, data marts are developed independently and independent teams work on the several data marts.

As already discussed, building independent data marts results in early delivery. This mitigates two pressures that development teams are under, (a) meet information needs early and (b) show that financial investment made is providing returns. As a result, there is great momentum behind building data marts as and when needed, with minimal concern for the enterprise data warehouse. Since departments gain early benefit from this, data mart proliferation has come to be widely accepted. Further, since data marts are developed taking only departmental requirements into account, they facilitate departmental control and better response times to queries. However, the downside of this is that independent data marts lead to the creation of departmental data silos [14–16]. That is, data needs of individual departments are satisfied but the data is not integrated across all the departments. This leads to data having inconsistent definitions, inconsistent collection and update times, and difficult sharing and integration.

Data mart proliferation raises a number of issues as follows:

- A large number of data marts imply increased hardware and software costs as well as higher support and maintenance costs.
- Each data mart has its own ETL process and so there are several such processes in a business.
- Same data existing in a large number of data marts leads to redundancy and inconsistency between data.
- There is no common data model. Multiple data definitions, differing update cycles, and differing data sources abound. This leads to inconsistent/inaccurate reports and analyses.
- Due to lack of consistency between similar data, it could happen that decision-making is inaccurate or inconsistent.

Data mart proliferation can be a drain on company resources. Industry surveys [14] show that the number of data marts maintained by 59% of companies is 30. There are companies that maintain 100 or more data marts. Maintenance of a single data mart can cost between $1.5 million and $2 million annually. Out of these costs, 35–70% are redundant costs.

The foregoing implies that there is a tipping point beyond which independent data mart proliferation becomes very expensive. Beyond this stage, an enterprise-wide data warehouse supporting dependent data marts can meet demand better. This is because such a data warehouse has enterprise scope, and therefore (a) supports multiple work areas and applications across the business, and (b) has consistent definitions of the data. The dependent data mart approach enables faster delivery than building yet another independent data mart does because new applications can leverage on the data in the data warehouse. It follows that at this tipping point, consolidating the disparate data marts together starts to create value.

Data mart consolidation involves building a centralized enterprise data warehouse (EDW). Data from multiple, disparate sources is centralized or consolidated into a single EDW. Anyone in the organization authorized to access data in the EDW will be able to do so. Thus, consolidation allows business to (a) retain functional capabilities of the original sources, and at the same time (b) broaden the business value of the data. Data mart consolidation provides benefits as follows:

- A centralized EDW results in common resources like hardware used, software and tools, processes, and personnel. This results in a significant reduction in cost per data mart.
- Since it is easier to secure centralized data than data distributed across different platforms in multiple locations, better information security can be provided. This also aids in being compliant with regulatory norms.
- There is a "single version of the truth", which enables better decision-making by providing more relevant information. Enterprise managers, as different from department managers, require data from all departments and this is made possible by data consolidation.

There are two factors in consolidation, the data warehouse implementation platform and the data model. This yields four possible approaches to doing consolidation:

1. Platform change but no change in data models: This addresses only the issues of consolidating the platform. All existing data marts are brought to the same platform. We get same common procedures for backup, recovery, and security. Proliferation of platforms and associated hardware/software costs is mitigated. Further, the business gets cost savings in supporting and maintenance staff. However, this is a mere re-hosting of existing data models and several data models continue to exist though on a centralized platform.
   This form of consolidation is relatively easy to carry through. The main effort lies in redoing those procedures that might have used platform-specific features. However, with this approach, multiple ETL processes continue to be needed and there is no metadata integration.
2. No platform change but changed data model: This type of consolidation does integrating of data of the several data marts. As a result, problems of inconsistency, redundancy, missing data, etc. are removed. BI applications give better

results and costs in keeping redundant data are minimized. This approach requires the construction of the bus of conformed dimensions. These may have not been determined earlier, as is likely in the approach of using Scrum and user stories, or consolidation may have been designed for, as in the approach of BEAM*. Clearly, the former shall require more work than the latter.

To the extent that conformed dimensions are used, some standardization of metadata does occur in this approach. However, non-conformed data continues to have different metadata. There could be changes in schemas due to conformed dimensions and these may require changes in the ETL processes. However, such changes are minimal. Similarly, there may be changes in the code that produces reports to take into account the changed schema.

Note, however, that due to diverse platforms, the cost savings of using a common platform do not accrue. According to [16] organizations use this as a first step in moving to consolidation as per approach (4) below.

3. No platform change, no change in data model: This leads to no consolidation and can be discarded.

4. Changed platform and changed data model. In this case, we get benefits of both a common platform and integrated data models. As mentioned earlier, this is the culminating step in data mart consolidation and is usually preceded by following approach (2) above.

   There are two ways in which this kind of consolidation can be done. These are as follows:

   a. Consolidate by merging with primary: Two data marts, a primary and a secondary data mart, are selected out of the several data marts that exist. The secondary data mart is to be merged with the primary. As a first step, the primary data mart is moved to the new platform. The secondary data mart is then migrated to the new platform and conformed to the primary or, in other words, conformed dimensions and facts are determined. Once merging is completed, the secondary data mart can be discarded. This migration to the new platform and integration with the primary is repeated for all remaining data marts to yield the enterprise-wide data warehouse.

      The "merge with primary" approach works well if the schema of the primary does not have to undergo major changes in accommodating the independent data marts. If this condition is not satisfied, then the approach considered below is deployed.

   b. Consolidate by doing a redesign: In this case, a fresh design is made keeping in mind the common information across independent data marts. Existing data marts are not used except to gain some understanding of the department view of the business, thereby laying a basis for development of the enterprise-wide data warehouse schema. Evidently, this approach can require large effort and time before delivery.

To sum up, the simplest form of data mart consolidation saves cost of software and hardware infrastructure. More complex forms of consolidation can further help in eliminating redundant and dormant processes ensuring a new optimized system. Data mart consolidation reaches fulfillment when it also removes inconsistencies and presents a "single version of the truth". When this happens, then the data warehouse addresses both departmental and enterprise-wide concerns. Through consolidation then, a stage is reached when functionality, processes, and hardware/software infrastructure are all rationalized.

2.6 Strategic Alignment

By strategic alignment, we refer to the alignment of a data warehouse with business strategy. This alignment is fostered when business and IT people come together with a realization that a data warehouse provides critical value to the organization and that the data warehouse can prove highly beneficial to the business. This means that the strategy for the deployment of IT should be co-developed with business strategy since IT processes play a major role in delivering business value.

In an aligned business, IT and business managers are jointly responsible for identifying IT investments to be made, prioritizing these, and deciding resource allocation. Since top business management is seen to be cooperating with IT managers, this cooperating culture flows down to all levels of the organization. As a result, there is effective communication to facilitate the realization of IT strategy and development of IT products and services by bringing together business and technological capabilities.

The foregoing is possible if there is corporate commitment at the top levels to alignment. On the other hand, IT professionals also need to learn the importance of alignment. Whereas, traditionally, the IT professional was largely evaluated on technical skills, today they need to additionally have skills for listening, negotiation and consensus building, teamwork, and customer service. The IT professional must be sensitive to the manner in which technology can be brought into the business, what benefits it can bring, and what changes in business practice will be needed. These new skills go a long way in developing cooperation with all stakeholders thereby minimizing conflict that may negatively affect IT plans.

We can now consider the alignment of data warehouse with business strategy. IT managers responsible for data warehousing must work together with business managers to achieve alignment. Alignment implies establishing coordination and communication besides doing joint envisioning of the data warehouse strategy and setting priorities. This is built on the basis that both IT and Business see the data warehouse as a critical resource that shall provide competitive advantage to the company.

Bansali [17] proposes five factors that apply specifically to alignment of data warehouse with business. These are as follows:

1. **Joint responsibility between data warehouse and business managers**: Since data warehousing involves multiple stakeholders each having their own data,

severe data quality issues emerge that need to be resolved. Senior management needs to impose data standards and additionally, overcome any resistance to change current practice.

2. **Alignment between data warehouse plan and business plan**: The vision of the data warehouse in the business needs to be defined. If this is only a short-term vision, then a lower budget will be allocated, early delivery shall be required, and the independent data mart approach shall be adopted. If on the other hand full organizational control is needed, then an enterprise-wide data warehouse would be required. The strategy for this may be through building data marts and then doing consolidation.

3. **Flexibility in data warehouse planning**: If there is likelihood that business strategy changes even as data warehouse development is ongoing, then a change in the business requirements of the data warehouse could be necessitated. In such a situation, iterative development with short lead times to delivery may be the answer.

4. **Technical integration of the data warehouse**: The business case for a data warehouse must first be established and business needs determined before opting for a particular technology. Selecting technology is based on its ability to address business and user requirements. The inability of the organization to absorb large amounts of new technology may lead to failure. Conversely, deploying old technology may not produce the desired results. Similarly, dumping huge quantities of new data in the lap of users may be as negative as providing very little new data.

5. **Business user satisfaction**: End-user participation is essential so as to both manage user expectations and satisfy their requirements. The selection of appropriate users in the project team is crucial.

The data warehouse community has responded to the need for alignment in several ways. One is the adoption of agile techniques. The agile manifesto is in four statements as follows:

- Individuals and interactions over processes and tools,
- Working software over comprehensive documentation,
- Customer collaboration over contract negotiation, and
- Responding to change over following a plan.

It can be seen that this manifesto addresses the five factors discussed above.

Agile development, as we have already seen, provides a broad developmental approach to data warehouse development but does not provide techniques by which the various stages shall be handled in a real project. To realize its full potential, it relies on models, tools, and techniques in the area of requirements, design, and construction engineering. Of interest to us, in this book, is requirements engineering. All work in the area of data warehouse requirements engineering, DWRE, is predicated upon close requirements engineer–stakeholder interaction.

2.7 Data Warehouse Requirements Engineering

The importance of requirements gathering was highlighted in Sect. 2.2. The area of data warehouse requirements engineering, DWRE, aims to arrive at a clear requirements specification on which both organizational stakeholders and the development team agree. As already seen, this specification may be a complete enterprise-wide specification if the DWSDLC is being followed breadth first, or it may be partial if the DWSDLC is being sliced vertically.

The first question that arises is, "what is a data warehouse requirement?" Notionally, this question can be answered in two ways:

(a) What shall the data warehouse do?
(b) What information shall the data warehouse provide?

Data warehouse technology does not directly address the first question. One answer that is provided is that the data warehouse supports analysis of different forms, analyze sales, analyze customer response, etc. The second answer is that the data warehouse can be queried, mined, and Online Analytical Processing (OLAP) operations performed on it. It follows that a data warehouse per se does not provide value to the business. Rather, value is obtained because of the improved decision-making that results from the better information that is available in it. This situation is different from that in transactional systems. These systems provide functionality and can perform actions. Thus, a hotel reservation system can do room bookings, cancelations, and the like. On the other hand, by providing capabilities to query, mine, and do OLAP, a data warehouse can be used by decision-makers to make decisions about what to do next. Therefore, data warehouse requirements cannot be expressed in terms of the functionality they provide, because they are not built to provide functionality. Asking what data warehouses do is the wrong question to ask.

The second question is of relevance to data warehousing. If the information to be kept in the data warehouse is known, then it is possible to structure it in multidimensional form and thereafter, to query it, mine it, and do OLAP with it. Thus, the data warehouse requirements engineering problem is that of determining the information contents of the data warehouse to-be. Again notice, the difference with transactional systems where supplying information is not the priority, and asking what information to keep would be the wrong question to ask.

Now, the information to be kept in the data warehouse cannot be determined in isolation and requires a context within which it is relevant. Thus, information for a human resource data mart is different from that of the finance data mart. Due to this, requirements engineering techniques explore the context and then arrive at the information that is to be kept in the data warehouse. There are several proposals for exploring the context and determining information relevant to the context.

Broadly speaking, there are two approaches as shown in Fig. 2.6. On the left side of the figure, we see that interest is in the immediate concern that motivates obtaining information from the data warehouse. This may be a requirement for analyzing sales, forecasting sales, or simply asking questions about sales. Once these needs are identified, then it is a matter of eliciting the information that should be kept in the data warehouse. The important point to note is that though the immediate context may be derived from an organizational one, the latter is not modeled and is only informally explored.

The second approach is shown on the right side of Fig. 2.6. Here, the organizational context that raises the immediate concern is also of interest and is, consequently, modeled. There is a clear representation of the organizational context from which the immediate context can be derived. For example, forecasting sales may be of interest because the organization is launching a variant of an existing product. It may also be interest to know trends of sales of existing products. The organizational context then provides the rationale for the immediate context. It provides a check that the immediate context is indeed relevant to the organization and is not merely a fanciful analysis.

How many levels deep is the organizational context? We will show that there are proposals for organizing data warehouse requirements engineering in multiple levels of the organizational context.

Immediate Context

Hughes [2] makes a case for agile data warehouse engineering and builds user stories that form the basis for subsequent data warehouse development. User stories principally specify the analysis needs of decision-makers, for example, analyze sales. This is determined by moving down the epic–theme–story levels of Scrum. The technique is completely based on interviewing and deriving stories.

Paim and Castro [18] proposed the DWARF technique and used traditional techniques like interviews and prototyping to elicit requirements.

Winter and Strauch [19] propose a cyclic process which maps the information demand made by middle-level managers and knowledge workers with information supplied in operational databases, reports, etc. They have an "initial" phase, an "as is" phase, and a "to be" phase. In the first phase, they argue that since different users can result in different data models, the dominant users must be identified. This helps

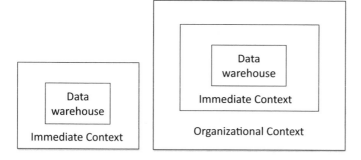

Fig. 2.6 Contexts of DWRE

target a specific business process. In the "as is" phase, an information map is created by analyzing (a) existing information systems and (b) reports that the users commonly use. According to the authors, analyzing the latter helps identify more sources of information that one is not commonly aware of. In the "to be" phase, information demand is elicited from the user by asking business questions. The information supply and information demand are compared and inconsistencies analyzed. Finally, using semantic models information requirements are modeled.

Organizational-Immediate Context

Traditionally, there are two major approaches: one is for setting the organizational context with goal modeling and the other with business process modeling. There is a third group of techniques that modify goal orientation by introducing additional business-related concepts. We refer to these as goal-motivated techniques.

As we have already seen, there is much interest in RE for transactional systems on goal-oriented [20, 21] and scenario-oriented techniques [22, 23]. These were coupled together to yield the goal–scenario coupling technique [24, 25]. Goal orientation uses means–ends analysis to reduce goals and the goal hierarchy identifies the goals that are to be operationalized in the system. Notice the near absence of the data/information aspect in goal orientation. Scenario orientation reveals typical functionality and its variations by identifying typical interaction between the system and the user. Even though example data is shown to flow across the system–user interface, focus is not on the data aspect; data and its modeling are largely ignored in scenario-oriented RE. Goal–scenario coupling allows development of a scenario for a goal of the goal hierarchy. Consequently, variations of goals are discovered in its scenario. Any new functionality indicated by the scenario is then introduced in the goal hierarchy. Thus, a mutually cooperating system is developed to better discover system goals. Again, notice that data is largely ignored.

A number of proposals for goal-oriented data warehouse requirements engineering, GODWRE, are available and all of these link goals with data, that is, all are aimed at obtaining facts and dimensions of data warehouses from goals [7, 26–31]. We consider each of these in turn.

The second approach takes business processes as the basis for determining the organizational context. An example of a business process is order processing. Events that take place during a business process generate/capture data and a business would like to analyze this data. Thus, data may be, for example, logs of web service execution, application logs, event logs, resource utilization data, financial data, etc. Interest is in analyzing the data to optimize processes, resource allocation, load prediction and optimization, and exception understanding and prevention.

When starting off from business processes, the several processes carried out in a business are first prioritized and the process to be taken up next is selected.

Requirements of the business process are then obtained and taken into one or more dimensional models.

The data resulting from events of business processes is essentially performance metrics and can be mapped to facts of the multidimensional model, whereas parameters of analysis become dimensions. Therefore, business intelligence can be applied to this data.

There are also a number of hybrid approaches that follow from goal-oriented approaches, one of which is to couple goals and processes. Others are for example to couple goals with key performance indicators and to couple goals with decisions. We refer to these as approaches that are motivated by goal modeling.

We consider these three types of DWRE techniques in the rest of this section.

2.7.1   Goal-Oriented DWRE Techniques

Goal-Oriented DWRE, GODWRE, techniques draw heavily from the notion of goals developed in GORE considered in Chap. 1. Thus, the organizational context of the data warehouse is represented in terms of goals that the business wants to achieve. Goal reduction techniques as in GORE are adopted to yield the goal hierarchy. Thereafter, facts and dimensions are associated with goals.

An early proposal for GODWRE was due to Bonifati et al. [27] who obtained DW structures from users' goals and operational databases. This was done by three levels of analysis: (i) top-down using goals, (ii) bottom-up for operational databases, and (iii) integration for integrating data warehouse structures obtained from steps (i) and (ii). Our interest is in step (i) only that relies on Goal–Question–Metric analysis.

Users' requirements are collected through traditional techniques like interviewing and brainstorming to obtain goals. A goal is expressed in terms of

- Object of study: the part of the reality being studied,
- Purpose: why the study is being done,
- Quality focus: the characteristics of interest in the study,
- Viewpoints: who is interested in the study, and
- Environment: the application context in which the study is being done.

Goals are further decomposed into simpler subgoals using goal reduction techniques.

Now, in order to obtain the information contents of the data warehouse, goal characteristics are collected on *GQM Abstraction sheets*. These sheets are in four parts as follows:

(a) Quality focus: The interesting question here is, "How can the quality focus be detailed?" There is no guidance on how to obtain these details but some examples are provided. These are cost, performance, resources required, etc. These factors yield the facts of the data warehouse to-be.

(b) Variation factor: The relevant question to ask here is, "What factors can influence quality focus?" Examples of such factors are customers, time, work center, etc. Again, eliciting variation factors requires considerably skilled and experienced requirements engineers who ask the right questions and understand the responses.

(c) Baseline hypothesis: What are the values assigned to the quality focus of interest? These are the typical queries that shall be asked when the warehouse becomes operational, for example, average cost of activities of a certain type.

(d) Impact on baseline hypothesis: How do baseline hypothesis vary quality focus? These tell us the query results that the data warehouse will produce once it becomes operational.

The requirements engineering aspect is over once abstraction sheets are built. However, just to complete the description of the technique, we consider the manner in which the star schema is constructed. First, using the information obtained from abstraction sheets, *ideal star schemas* are constructed. Thereafter, in the bottom-up analysis phase, step (ii) above, entity relationship diagrams of existing operational databases are obtained and converted to star schemas. Finally, in step (iii) the ideal star schemas and those of step (ii) are matched. A metrics for selection is applied and the star schemas are ranked. The designer then chooses the best fit for system design.

Notice that in this technique, the organization context is the goal structure, whereas the immediate context is the abstraction sheets.

Yet, another goal-oriented technique is due to Mazon et al. [30] who base their approach on i* methodology. They relate goals supported by DW with information requirements. Facts and dimensions are discovered from information requirements.

An intentional actor refers to a decision-maker involved in the decision-making process. For each intentional actor, there are three intentional elements *goals, tasks,* and *resources*. *Goals* can be of three kinds:

- *Strategic goals* are at the highest level of abstraction. These goals are the main objectives of the business process and cause a beneficial change of state in the business. Thus, increase sales is a strategic goal.
- *Decision goals* are at the next lower level of abstraction. These goals are for achieving strategic goals. As an example, "open new store" is a decision goal that achieves the strategic goal and increases sales.
- *Information goals* are at the lowest level of abstraction. These goals identify the information required to achieve a decision goal. For example, "analyze purchases" is an information goal.

Information is derived from information goals and is represented as tasks that must be carried out to achieve information goals.

The requirements process starts with identification of decision-makers and a strategic dependency model is built that shows the dependency between different decision-makers. In the Strategic Rationale model, SR of i*, specific concepts for multidimensional structures are introduced. These are business process, measures, and context. Business processes are related to goals of decision-makers, measures are related to the information obtained from information goals, and context is the way in which information is analyzed. Relations between contexts are defined that enable aggregates to be determined.

We can summarize the steps to be carried out as follows:

- Discovering the intentional actors, i.e., the decision-makers and defining SR models for each decision-maker;
- Discovering the three kinds of goals of decision-makers;
- From information goals discovered, arriving at information requirements; and
- Extracting multidimensional concepts from information requirements.

This basic technique has been used by Leal et al. [32] to develop a business strategy based approach. The basic idea is to go deeper into the organizational context. Thus, we can consider the proposal to be the introduction of another layer, the business strategic layer as shown in Fig. 2.7.

The new layer is for VMOST analysis of the business, vision, mission, objective, strategy, and tactic. First, decision-makers are identified. The DW is also considered as an actor. VMOST components along with strategic goals are obtained from decision-makers. Thereafter, intentional elements like objectives, tasks, and tactics are elicited as are means–ends links. After verifying that the VMOST components are in accordance with the BMM model concepts, the approach of strategic, decision, and information goals outlined above is followed.

The GRAND approach [31, 33] divides the requirements elicitation process into two perspectives, the organizational perspective and the decisional perspective. The former models the requirements of the business that includes actors who may not be decision-makers. This perspective consists of two steps, goal analysis and fact analysis. In the goal analysis phase, goals for the actor are represented using an actor diagram. Each goal is decomposed by AND/OR decomposition and the rationale diagram built. During the facts analysis phase, facts are associated with

Fig. 2.7 The business strategic layer

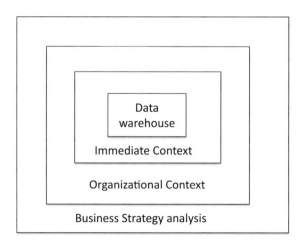

goals. This association arises because facts are the data to be kept when a goal is achieved. Finally, facts are augmented with their attributes.

In the decisional phase, the organizational model is reviewed but with the decision-maker as the actor. The focus in this phase is in determining the analysis needs of the decision-maker and goals like analyze sales are established. Such goals are decomposed to yield their own goal hierarchy. Facts are normally imported from the organizational perspective but some additional facts may be obtained when the analyst investigates the goal model of the decisional phase. Dimensions are obtained by considering the leaf goals of the decision-maker goal hierarchy and the facts in the upper layers of this hierarchy.

2.7.2   Goal-Motivated Techniques

The techniques discussed in the previous section associate facts and dimensions with goals. There are other approaches that start out with goals but introduce an intermediate concept using which facts and dimensions are obtained.

The goal-process approach of Boehnlein and Ulbricht [7, 26] rely on the Semantic Object model, SOM, framework. After building a goal model for the business at hand, the business processes that are performed to meet the goals are modeled. The business application systems resulting from these are then used to yield a schema in accordance with the Structured Entity Relationship Model, SERM. Business objects of the business processes get represented as entities of SERM, and dependencies between entities are derived from the task structure. Thereafter, a special fourth stage is added to SOM in which only those attributes that are relevant for information analysis required for decision-making are identi-fied. Thereafter, the developer converts the SERM schema to facts and dimensions; facts are determined by asking the question, how can goals be evaluated by metrics? Dimensions are identified from dependencies of the SERM schema.

The Goal-Decision-Information, GDI, technique [28, 29] associates decisions with business goals. A decision is a selection from a choice set of alternative. Each alternative is a way of achieving a goal. The decision-maker needs information in order to select an alternative. For each decision, relevant information is obtained by writing informational scenarios. These scenarios are sequences of information requests expressed in an SQL-like language. An information scenario is thus a typical system–stakeholder interaction to identify information required for a deci-sion. Once information for all decisions is elicited, an ER diagram is built from which the multidimensional schema is constructed.

Typical information retrieval requests use the rather fuzzy notion of "relevant information". What constitutes "relevance" is not spelt out.

2.7.3   Miscellaneous Approaches

Though the DWRE area is highly oriented toward goals, techniques that start off from notions other than goals do exist.

One such example is that of BEAM*. This approach [12] gives prominence to business events that comprise a business process. Each business event is represented as a table and the RE problem now is to identify the table attributes. This is done by using the 7W framework that provides for asking questions of seven types, namely, (1) Who is involved in the event? (2) What did they do? To what is done? (3) When did it happen? (4) Where did it take place? (5) Why did it happen? (6) How did it happen—in what manner? and (7) How many or much was recorded —how can it be measured? Out of these, the first six supply dimensions, whereas the last one supplies facts.

Yet, another proposal kicks off from use cases [34]. Use cases are used for communication between stakeholders, domain experts, and DW designers. The authors propose an incremental method to develop use cases. Facade iteration is the first iteration where use case outlines and high-level descriptions are captured. Its purpose is to identify actors for other major iterations. The information gathered is regarding names and short descriptions of actor interactions with DW system.

During the next iteration, ideas of use cases are broadened and deepened. They generally include "functional", information requirements plus requirement attributes. Since the requirements gathered can be too large, use cases are first individually evaluated for errors and omissions, then prioritized and pruned. This is done so that at the end only the use cases that provide sufficient information to build DW system are left. Thereafter, conflicting/inconsistent use cases are identified and reassessed. Finally, use cases are used for obtaining relevant information.

The use of key performance indicators has also formed the basis of DWRE techniques. References [35, 36] model business indicators as functions and identify the needed parameters and return type. That is, input and output information needed to compute a business indicator is determined.

2.7.4   Obtaining Information

It can be seen that there is a clear attempt to obtain the context in which facts and dimensions of interest carry meaning. This context is explored through a variety of concepts like goals, decisions, business processes, business events, and KPIs. Thereafter, attention turns to obtaining data warehouse information. The techniques for this second part are summarized in Table 2.4.

The primary difficulty with Boehnlein and Ulbricht is the absence of any model or guideline to discover the attributes relevant to the analysis. The authors do not indicate how stakeholders articulate the analysis to be performed. Consequently, attribute identification becomes an unfocused activity. Further, the approach is for

Table 2.4 Approaches to obtaining information

Approach	Obtaining data warehouse information
Boehnlein and Ulbricht	• Relevant business objects and attributes • Edges of SERM schema
Bonifati	Quality focus and variation factors
Prakash and Gosain	Information scenarios
Mazón et al.	Measures, context
Georgini et al.	Goal achievement measures, dimensions from leaves of goal hierarchy
Nasiri et al. [37]	Follows approach of Mazón et al. as in row 4 of this table
Corr and Stagnitto	Uses 7W framework

obtaining "nominal" information for the company as a whole. Therefore, individual stakeholder's information needs are de-emphasized.

Bonifati relies on quality focus and variation factors. Evidently merely asking questions like "how quality focus can be detailed" and "what factors can influence quality focus" is not enough since no guidance and support is provided for answering the questions. We need some model that can be populated and a suitable investigation needs to be carried out to perform this task.

Even though an SQL-like structure of queries is provided to express information scenarios by Prakash and Gosain, there is no guidance on what information to ask for and what factors to consider. Thus, the approach relies heavily on the experience of the scenario writer.

Mazón et al. rely on obtaining measures and contexts for information goals. This is an ad hoc activity that relies completely on stakeholder experience.

Georgini et al., similarly, do not provide guidance in the task of analyzing leaf goals and on the aspects to be considered in arriving at dimensions.

The last row of Table 2.4 deals with the 7W framework used in Corr and Stagnitto. This approach is rather simplistic; compared to this, the other techniques discussed here provide some concepts using which stakeholders can identify their information needs.

2.8   Conclusion

Data warehouse development has two major concerns, namely

1. What method to adopt to build data warehouses without imposing excessive costs on organizations and minimizing the lead times for product delivery? This is the issue of the development strategy to be adopted.
2. How to ensure that the data warehouse to-be meets the information requirements of decision-makers? This is the issue of requirements engineering.

As for transactional systems, the two issues have been treated independently of one another. That is, the manner in which requirements engineering can support an efficient, iterative, and incremental development strategy has not been addressed.

It is evident, however, that there is a fundamental difference between requirements engineering for transactional systems and that for data warehousing. The former is oriented toward discovering the functionality of the system to-be. The discovered functionality is then implemented or operationalized in the system to be built. In contrast, the problem of DWRE is to determine the information contents of the data warehouse to-be. However, our analysis of information elicitation techniques shows that these are rather ad hoc, and provide little guidance in the requirements engineering task. We need models, tools, and techniques to do this task better.

References

1. Loshin, D. (2013). *Business intelligence the savvy manager's guide* (2nd ed.). Elsevier.
2. Hughes, R. (2013). *Agile data warehousing project management business intelligence systems using scrum*. Morgan Kaufman.
3. Ericson, J. (2006, April). *A simple plan, information management magazine*. http://www.information-management.com/issues/20060401/1051182-1.html. Accessed September 2011.
4. Hayen, R., Rutashobya, C., & Vetter, D. (2007). An investigation of the factors affecting data warehousing success. *Issues In Information Systems, VIII*(2), 547–553.
5. Alshboul, R. (2012). Data warehouse explorative study. *Applied Mathematical Sciences, 6* (61), 3015–3024.
6. Inmon, B. (2005). *Building the data warehouse* (4th ed.). New York: Wiley.
7. Boehnlein, M., & Ulbrich vom Ende, A. (1999). Deriving initial data warehouse structures from the conceptual data models of the underlying operational information systems. In *Proceedings of Workshop on Data Warehousing and OLAP* (pp. 15–21). ACM.
8 Hüsemann, B., Lechtenbörger, J., & Vossen, G. (2000). Conceptual data warehouse design. In *Proceedings of the International Workshop on Design and Management of Data Warehouses (DMDW'2000), Stockholm, Sweden, June 5–6*.
9 Moody, L.D., & Kortink, M.A.R. (2000). From enterprise models to dimensional models: A methodology for data warehouses and data mart design. In *Proceedings of the International Workshop on Design and Management of Data Warehouses, Stockholm, Sweden* (pp. 5.1–5.12)
10. Golfarelli, M., Maio, D., & Rizzi, S. (1998). Conceptual design of data warehouses from E/R schemes. In *Proceedings of the Thirty-First Hawaii International Conference on System Sciences, 1998* (Vol. 7, pp. 334–343). IEEE.
11. Prakash, N., Prakash, D., & Sharma, Y. K. (2009). Towards better fitting data warehouse systems. In *The practice of enterprise modeling* (pp. 130–144). Springer, Berlin, Heidelberg.
12. Corr, L., & Stagnitto, J. (2012). *Agile data warehouse design*. UK: Decision One Press.
13. Ambler, S. www.agiledata.org.
14. CMP. *Data mart consolidation* and *business intelligence standardization*. www.businessobjects.com/pdf/investors/data_mart_consolidation.pdf.
15. Muneeswara, P. C. *Data mart consolidation process, What, Why, When, and How, Hexaware Technologies white paper*. www.hexaware.com.
16. Ballard, C., Gupta A., Krishnan V., Pessoa N., & Stephan O. *Data mart consolidation: Getting control of your enterprise information*. redbooks.ibm.com/redbooks/pdfs/sg246653.pdf.

17. Bansali, N. (2007). *Strategic alignment in data warehouses two case studies* (Ph.D. thesis). RMIT University.
18. Paim, F. R. S., & de Castro, J. F. B. (2003). DWARF: An approach for requirements definition and management of data warehouse systems. In *11th IEEE Proceedings of International Conference on Requirements Engineering, 2003* (pp. 75–84). IEEE.
19. Winter, R., & Strauch, B. (2003). A method for demand-driven information requirements analysis in data warehousing projects. In *Proceedings of the 36th Annual Hawaii International Conference on System Sciences, 2003* (p. 9). IEEE.
20. Antón, A. I. (1996, April). Goal-based requirements analysis. In *Proceedings of the Second International Conference on Requirements Engineering* (pp. 136–144). IEEE.
21. Lamsweerde, A. (2000). Requirements engineering in the year 00: A research perspective. In *Proceedings of the 22nd International Conference on Software Engineering* (pp. 5–19). ACM.
22. Sutcliffe, A. G., Maiden, N. A., Minocha, S., & Manuel, D. (1998). Supporting scenario-based requirements engineering. *IEEE Transactions on Software Engineering, 24* (12), 1072–1088.
23. Lamsweerde, A., & Willemet, L. (1998). Inferring declarative requirements specifications from operational scenarios. *IEEE Transactions on Software Engineering, 24*(12), 1089–1114.
24. CREWS Team. (1998). The CREWS glossary, CREWS Report 98-1. http://SUNSITE. informatik.rwth-aachen.de/CREWS/reports.htm.
25. Liu, L., & Yu, E. (2004). Designing information systems in social context: A goal and scenario modelling approach. *Information systems, 29*(2), 187–203.
26. Boehnlein, M., & Ulbrich vom Ende, A. (2000). Business process oriented development of data warehouse structures. In *Proceedings of Data Warehousing 2000* (pp. 3–21). Physica Verlag HD.
27. Bonifati, A., Cattaneo, F., Ceri, S., Fuggetta, A., & Paraboschi, S. (2001). Designing data marts for data warehouses. *ACM Transactions on Software Engineering and Methodology, 10* (4), 452–483.
28. Prakash, N., & Gosain, A. (2003). Requirements driven data warehouse development. In *CAiSE Short Paper Proceedings* (pp. 13–17).
29. Prakash, N., & Gosain, A. (2008). An approach to engineering the requirements of data warehouses. *Requirements Engineering Journal, Springer, 13*(1), 49–72.
30. Mazón, J. N., Pardillo, J., & Trujillo, J. (2007). A model-driven goal-oriented requirement engineering approach for data warehouses. *Advances in Conceptual Modeling–Foundations and Applications* (pp. 255–264). Springer, Berlin, Heidelberg.
31. Giorgini, P., Rizzi, S., & Garzetti, M. (2008). GRAnD: A goal-oriented approach to requirement analysis in data warehouses. *Decision Support Systems, 45*(1), 4–21.
32. Leal, C. A., Mazón, J. N., & Trujillo, J. (2013). A business-oriented approach to data warehouse development. *Ingeniería e Investigación, 33*(1), 59–65.
33. Giorgini, P., Rizzi, S., & Garzetti, M. (2005). Goal-oriented requirement analysis for data warehouse design. In *Proceedings of the 8th ACM International Workshop on Data Warehousing and OLAP* (pp. 47–56). ACM.
34. Bruckner, R., List, B., & Scheifer, J. (2001). Developing requirements for data warehouse systems with use cases. In *AMCIS 2001 Proceedings*, 66.
35. Prakash, N., & Bhardwaj, H. (2014). Functionality for business indicators in data warehouse requirements engineering. *Advances in conceptual modeling* (pp. 39–48). Springer International Publishing.
36. Bhardwaj, H., & Prakash, N. (2016). Eliciting and structuring business indicators in data warehouse requirements engineering. *Expert Systems, 33*(4), 405–413.
37. Nasiri, A., Wrembel, R., & Zimányi, E. (2015). Model-based requirements engineering for data warehouses: From multidimensional modelling to KPI monitoring. In *International Conference on Conceptual Modeling* (pp. 198–209). Springer.

Chapter 3
Issues in Data Warehouse Requirements Engineering

In this chapter, we consider the three issues that emerge from the previous chapter, namely,

1. The need for a central notion that forms the focus of data warehouse requirements engineering. Just as the notion of a function is central to transactional requirements engineering, we propose the concept of a decision as the main concept for data warehouse requirements engineering.
2. The development of information elicitation techniques. The absence of systematic information elicitation makes the data warehouse requirements engineering process largely ad-hoc. We propose to systemize these techniques.
3. The tension between rapid DW fragment development and consolidation. This tension arises because consolidation is treated as a project in itself separate from the DW fragment development process. We propose to integrate it with the requirements engineering process of the data warehouse development life cycle.

3.1 The Central Notion of a Decision

Since a data warehouse system is used to provide support for decision-making, our premise is that any model that is developed must be rooted in the essential nature of decision-making. Therefore, in this section, we first consider the notion of a decision process. Thereafter, we consider the role of data warehousing in decision-making and highlight the importance of basing data warehouse requirements engineering on the notion of a decision.

© Springer Nature Singapore Pte Ltd. 2018
N. Prakash and D. Prakash, *Data Warehouse Requirements Engineering*,
https://doi.org/10.1007/978-981-10-7019-8_3

3.1.1 The Decision Process

The decision process, see Fig. 3.1, can be seen as transforming information as input into decisions as outputs. The input/output nature of a decision process suggests information transfer to and from elements that are external to the process. These elements may be sub-processes within the same decision system or may be separate elements. These elements are collectively referred to as the environment of the decision process. It is important for the environment and the decision process to be appropriately matched so as to achieve the intended purpose.

The decision-making process has been described in terms of (a) its essential nature and (b) the steps that constitute it. According to the former, **decision-making** is [1], the intellectual task of selecting a particular course of action from a set of alternative courses of action. This set of alternatives is often referred to as the choice set. Turban [2] takes this further. Not only is an alternative selected but there is also commitment to the selected course of action. Makarov et al. [3] formulate the decision-making problem as an optimization problem and the idea is to pick up the most optimal alternative from the choice set. Given C, a set of alternatives, and Op as an optimality principle, the decision-making problem is represented as the pair <C, Op>. The decision-maker is the person, a manager in an organization perhaps, who formulates this pair and thereafter finds its solution. The solution to <C, Op> is the set of alternative(s), C_{Op}, that meet the optimality principle Op.

The second view of the decision-making process emphasizes the steps to be followed in performing this task. Simon [4] considers these steps as decision-making phases. There are three phases:

- Intelligence: This is for searching conditions that need decisions,
- Design: Possible courses of action are identified in this phase. This may require inventing, developing, and analyzing courses of actions, and
- Choice: Here, selection of a course of action is done from those available.

A more detailed description of the decision-making process is available in [5]. The decision-making process is organized here in five steps as follows:

(1) Define the problem,
(2) Identify the alternatives and criteria, constituting the decision problem. That is, C and Op of the <C, Op> pair are identified,
(3) Build an evaluation matrix for estimating the alternatives criteria-wise,
(4) Select method to be applied for doing decision-making, and
(5) Provide a final aggregated evaluation.

Fig. 3.1 The decision process

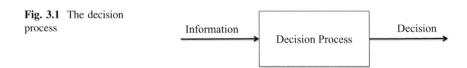

Information → Decision Process → Decision

Decision processes have been classified as well-structured, semi-structured, and ill-unstructured. Well-structured processes have three major characteristics, namely, that (a) it is possible to formulate a definite criterion for testing any proposed solution, (b) a problem space can be defined in which the initial state, the final state, and all possible transitions between these are available, and (c) it is possible to calculate all possible computations. Due to these characteristics, such processes can be reduced to well-defined rules and can therefore be automated. Computers can carry out well-structured process well, even better than human beings can.

Human beings are better than computers at dealing with ill-structured decision processes. Such processes may have ambiguous, imperfect or incomplete information, ill-defined, and/or conflicting goals. Therefore, ill-structured processes cannot be reduced to well-defined rules.

Semi-structured decision processes lie between well-structured and ill-structured ones. They can be decomposed into parts that are well-structured and others that are ill-structured. There are a number of methods for dealing with semi-structured processes:

(1) AHP (Analytic Hierarchy Process) [6]: In this method, a hierarchy is built that consists of the goal of the process as the root node. The alternatives are at the leaf nodes of the hierarchy. The criteria for selection are nodes at levels between the root and the leaves. If criteria cannot be decomposed, then there is only one level between the leaves and the root, otherwise there can be several levels.

Priorities are assigned to nodes that weight them with values between 0 and 1. The root node has the value 1. Let us assume that criteria cannot be decomposed further and we have a three-level analytical hierarchy. Values assigned to criteria nodes add up to unity. A pair-wise comparison of "criteria" nodes is carried out to estimate the contribution made to the goal. This comparison yields the values to be assigned to each node. Similarly, a pair-wise comparison of "alternative" nodes is done to estimate the extent of fulfillment of each criterion. These values are then weighted according to the criteria weight to obtain the final value.

(2) MAUT (Multi-Attribute Utility Theory) [7] is a way of evaluating alternatives based on the attributes of these alternatives. It consists of a number of steps, (a) define the alternatives and relevant attributes and (b) evaluate each alternative on each attribute. If there is an alternative that is worse than another alternative on all attributes, then it is discarded because such an alternative will never be opted to (c) assign relative weights to the attributes and (d) combine the attribute weights and evaluations to yield an overall evaluation of each alternative.

(3) In order to judge if one alternative is "at least as good" as another alternative, outranking methods, exemplified by ELECTRE, raise the issue to whether enough information exists. The term, outranking, indicates the degree of dominance of one alternative over another.

Outranking methods start with a given set of distinct alternatives a_i, $1 \leq i$ n and a set of decision criteria g_j, $1 \leq j \geq p$. Further, $g_j(a_i)$ expresses the performance of alternative i on criterion j. Consider the performances $g_j(a_k)$ and $g_j(a_l)$ of two alternatives a_k and a_l on the criterion g_j. If these performance values are sufficiently close to each other, then it is difficult to differentiate between them, that is, the decision-maker is indifferent to them. If the difference between the performance values is sufficiently large, there is clarity on which is the better alternative. In between there is an area of weak preference. To represent this, a threshold model is defined that consists of two thresholds for the criterion j, the indifference and preference thresholds, q_j and p_j respectively. Thus, we get

$$a_k \text{ Indifferent to } a_l \text{ when } |g_j(a_k) - g_j(a_l)| \leq q_j$$
$$a_k \text{ Preferred to } a_l \text{ when } |g_j(a_k) - g_j(a_l)| > p_j$$
$$a_k \text{ weakly preferred to } a_l \text{ when } q_j \leq |g_j(a_k) - g_j(a_l)| \leq p_j$$

(4) Weighting methods [8]: Weighting methods are based on assignment of weights to the decision criteria to the decisional problem. It is assumed that all criteria are such that the higher the value, the better they are. Let the weight of importance of criteria j be w_j and let the performance value of an alternative a_i for j be a_{ij}. Then, the weighted sum score of the alternative a_i for all criteria is

$$a_i^{ws} = \sum_{j=1}^{n} w_j a_{ij} \text{ for all i}$$

When looking for maximization, the alternative with the highest weighted score is the best one.

(5) Fuzzy methods [9, 10] use fuzzy set theory to enrich decision-making methods for defining decision criteria and/or attributes values. As a result, uncertainty and interdependence between criteria and alternatives can be addressed. However, preferences determined by this type of methods can be inexact.

3.1.2 Decision-Oriented Data Warehousing

If we consider a data warehouse as a repository of organizational information, then the decision-making process is external to it. The role of the data warehouse is limited to providing information inputs to this process. This information could reflect the state of the business as obtained from transactional systems. It could also be aggregated or mined information obtained by processing transaction information. In all cases, a data warehouse is the source of information and it is for the external decision process to use this source to produce the decision output.

Evidently then, the data warehouse is neutral to whether the decision process is structured, ill-structured, or semi-structured. In its role as information supplier, the data warehouse must supply complete, unambiguous, and perfect information to structured decision processes. If the decision process is not well structured and the nature of information is a factor in this being so, then the information supplied may be incomplete, imperfect, and ambiguous. The data warehouse is not impacted by factors other than the nature of information and is thus neutral to unstructured processes arising, for example, due to ill-defined decision-making goals.

Whereas from the decision process viewpoint interest in a data warehouse is as a source of information to arrive at decisions, from the data warehouse requirements engineering, DWRE, point of view interest is in determining the information contents of the data warehouse to support decision-making. In other words, if we can determine the decisions of interest, then the requirements engineering task would be to discover the information relevant to these. The information may be well defined to support structured decision processes, or it may be insufficiently defined and support semi-structured decision processes (Fig. 3.2).

Since information discovery is motivated by decisions, we refer to this requirements engineering process as decision-centric. We see the decision-centric requirements engineering process in two parts:

1. Determination of decisions.
2. Elicitation of information relevant to each decision.

Evidently, it is not possible to claim that all possible decisions shall be determined. That is, the completeness of the set of decisions cannot be established but, in keeping with requirements engineering practice, an agreement can be reached among stakeholders and with the requirements engineer that the discovered ones are adequate.

We see three kinds of decisions in a business, namely, decisions for formulating business policies, for formulating policy enforcement rules, and for operational decision-making. Policies are the broad principles/directions that the business shall follow. Policies are relatively stable over time but change when the business or its environment changes. Policy enforcement rules provide guidelines/directives on possible actions that can be taken in given business situations and can be represented in the IF x THEN y, where x is a business situation and y is a possible course of action. Policy enforcement rules, PERs, can be formulated once policies are

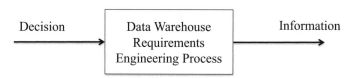

Fig. 3.2 Decision-centric requirements engineering

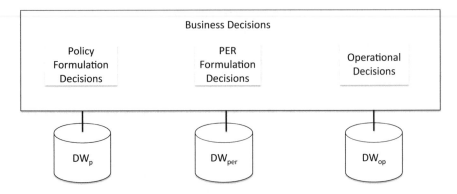

Fig. 3.3 Decision-centric data warehouses/marts

agreed upon. These rules change relatively more often than policies do. Finally, operational decisions are selections of possible courses of actions that can be implemented/carried out in the business.

Figure 3.3 shows an architecture for these three kinds of decisions. The rectangle at the top of the figure shows that a business consists of three different kinds of decisions. For each of these, we have a separate data warehouse/mart, DW_p for policy formulation decisions, DW_{per} for PER formulation, and DW_{op} for operational decisions, respectively.

Taken individually, each data warehouse/mart has its own decisional motivation. The kinds of decisions that are to be supported are different and each data warehouse has its own information contents. There is no common data model and common platform. However, from the point of view of an enterprise, the three kinds of business decisions are interrelated as shown in Fig. 3.4: policy decisions lead to decisions about policy enforcement rules that in turn lead to operational decisions. Let us illustrate this through an example of a hospital service.

Policy decisions lead to formulation of policies of the hospital. For example, in order to have an adequate number of doctors, the hospital defines patient: doctor ratios, eight patients for every doctor, twelve per doctor, etc. Once the policy has been laid down, rules to enforce it must be formulated. This is done through decisions for formulating PERs. Thus, see Fig. 3.4, PER decisions are **derived** from policy decisions. For example, in our hospital, patient demand for services, resignations and superannuation of doctors, enhancing services, etc. lead to situations in which the patient: doctor policy could be violated. PERs articulate the actions to be taken under given conditions, when to transfer doctors from one unit to another, when to hire, etc.

Lastly, Fig. 3.4 shows that PER decisions **drive** operational decisions. The issue in operational decision-making is that of first deciding the PER that shall be selected and thereafter, about the parameters/individuals on which the action of the selected rule shall be applied. For example, given the choice of hiring or transferring a

Fig. 3.4 Relationships
between decision types

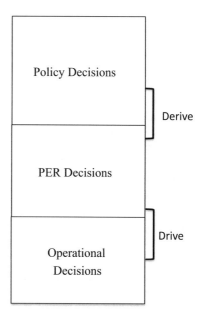

doctor, a decision about which one is to be adopted is needed. Let us say that it is to transfer. Thereafter, the particular doctor to be transferred is to be decided upon.

The forgoing suggests that policy and PER decisions do not cause changes in transactional data whereas operational decisions do. To see this, consider our hospital once again and refer to Fig. 3.5. As shown in the figure, transactional information systems supply information that shall be kept in the data warehouse. Before it is put in the data warehouse, the ETL (Extraction, Transformation, and Loading) process is carried out.

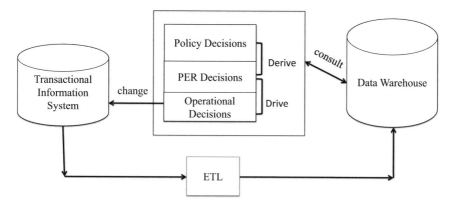

Fig. 3.5 The effect of decisions

Now, let it be required to take the decision that formulates the patient–doctor policy. The decision-maker consults the data warehouse before an appropriate patient: doctor ratio is adopted. As such, there is no effect on the transactional information system. When the decision-maker derives PERs from the policy, then again reference to the data warehouse is made. Yet again, there is no effect on the transactional information system. During operational decision-making, the decision-maker selects the appropriate PER to be applied to the situation at hand. Again, the data warehouse needs to be consulted to comprehend the current situation of the business. Even at this stage, the transactional information system shall not be affected. However, when the parameters/individuals of the action suggested by the rule are determined from the data warehouse and then the action is actually performed, then, and only then, shall the data in the transactional system be changed (for example, the unit of the doctor shall change upon transfer). This is shown in Fig. 3.5 by the arrow labeled change.

The relationship between the various kinds of decisions and therefore between their data warehouses (Fig. 3.3) indicates that an all-encompassing enterprise-wide data warehouse would support all three kinds of decision-making. In other words, we could treat the three individual data warehouses as well as their different components taken separately as DW fragments. The DW fragment proliferation problem therefore gets even more severe and special attention to consolidation needs to be paid.

Data Warehouse Fragments

It is to be noted that motivation behind the decisional data warehouse is not mere analysis but the idea of providing information support to a decision. This decision is the reason for doing analysis and analysis per se is not interesting. That is, the data warehouse is not developed based on perceived analysis needs; data warehousing is not driven by such statements as "I want to analyze sales" but by explicit decisions like "Arrest sales of mobile phones" and "Abandon land line telephony". Such decisions call for eliciting relevant information and making it available in the data warehouse/mart.

This decision-centric nature of the DWRE process changes the perspective of a DW and because of this shift, we postulate the notion of a data warehouse fragment. We define a **data warehouse fragment, DW fragment** for brevity, as a *decision-oriented* collection of time variant, nonvolatile, and integrated data. This is in contrast to a DW fragment being subject-oriented, time variant, nonvolatile, and integrated collection of data.

A subject-oriented data mart lays emphasis on the business unit (sales, purchase) for which the data warehouse is to be built. Interest is in determining the information relevant to the unit. During requirements elicitation, stakeholders identify what they want to analyze and what information is needed for this analysis. The reason behind doing this analysis remains in the background.

A DW fragment springs off from the decisions that it shall support. There are two aspects to be considered, decisions and information. Decisions may be completely local to a unit of an organization or may span across organizational units. In the former case, a DW fragment that supports departmental decision-making is developed whereas for the latter, an inter-departmental/enterprise-wide DW fragment is constructed.

DW fragments call for eliciting information relevant to decisions that the fragment aims to support and this information may be contained within an organizational unit or across units. Three cases arise as follows:

(a) If a decision taken by a unit needs information exclusively from the unit itself, then the requirements elicitation process is confined to the unit itself. All information sources/stakeholders are from the unit.
(b) If the decision taken by a unit requires information from multiple units, then the requirements elicitation process must identify these information sources/stakeholders to get the required information.
(c) The decision is to be taken by consensus across several units then, as for (b), information from multiple units is required.

In all these cases, it is apparent that the purpose of decision orientation is to directly relate the data warehouse to the useful work that it supports. Interest is in what managers can do with the DW fragment rather than merely on the nature of data it holds.

Since a DW fragment is defined with no reference to a subject, it can accommodate information about several subjects obtained from several units gracefully. The only requirement is that the information must be relevant to the decision-making task at hand. In contrast, data marts handle information from one unit per mart. Information across multiple units can only be handled by integrating/consolidating the multiple data marts but defining the subject for such marts can get difficult. For example, consolidation of the sales and purchase data marts leads to a new mart. The question, "What is the subject of the new data mart?" does not have a clear answer. Is it inventory control? Stores? Customer relationship?

Since a data mart is defined with no reference to the decisions that it supports, there is no clear articulation of what decision-makers can do with it. So, what information should a data mart contain? One possible answer is to put "all" information in it. After all, it can be argued, any piece of information may be needed at any time. The practical approach, however, is to leave it to the experience of the stakeholder to decide data mart information contents. In contrast, the DW fragment says that only that information which is relevant to the decision it supports has a place in it. If a new decision is to be supported, then a new DW fragment needs to be built.

A DW fragment is built for a decision or a collection of decisions (when fragment consolidation has occurred). Thus, we can have one-decision DW fragments, two-decision DW fragments, three-decision DW fragments, and so on. As for data marts, smaller DW fragments would need to be consolidated so as to eventually build the enterprise-wide data warehouse.

Proliferation of data marts/DW fragments is dependent upon their granularity. The bigger the granularity, the less is the amount of proliferation. For data marts, the bigger the subject, the less is the proliferation. Thus, a stores data mart has a larger granularity than the sales data mart or the purchase data mart. We get one mart for the subject store and two for the latter. Similarly, if a DW fragment is for a decision of large granularity or for several decisions, then we will get a larger DW fragment than if the fragment is for a small granularity decision. We will consider the notion of decision granularity in detail in Chap. 6.

3.2   Obtaining Information Requirements

The decision-centric DWRE process aims to discover the information relevant to each decision of interest. Evidently, this information shall be obtained from those stakeholders who are decision-makers in the organization. For the process to be effective, stakeholders must see their concerns being addressed by the data warehouse under development. Therefore, we consider here the factors that enhance stakeholder buy-in in the information elicitation process.

Interest of a decision-maker is in determining the gap between the current situation of an organization and the expected situation. The former is obtained by keeping a trace of organizational activities, and this trace is obtained from Online Transaction Processing, OLTP, systems that keep track of the transactions performed. The expected situation, on the other hand, lies in the intentions of managers: what does a manager want to achieve. First and foremost, a manager must be able to meet the goals set for him. Further, goals must be met efficiently and effectively. Having taken a decision that contributes to these broad objectives, the manager should be able to assess the impact of the decisions and this assessment may form the basis of subsequent decision-making. We propose four factors, one each for these four issues. This is summarized in Table 3.1.

We consider each row of Table 3.1 in turn.

3.2.1   Critical Success Factors

Bullen and Rockart [11] look upon a Critical Success Factor, CSF, as a key area of work. Meeting a CSF is essential for a manager to achieve his/her goals. Evidently,

Table 3.1 Managerial issues and associated factors

Driving force	Relevant factor
Success	Critical success factors
Effectiveness	Ends achievement, i.e., whether Ends have been achieved or not
Efficiency	Means efficiency, i.e., efficiency of the adopted means
Changing environment	Outcome feedback

a manager should have full information to determine if work is proceeding well in the area of the CSF. Wetherbe points out that most managers have only a few critical success factors, typically 4–8 [12]. Bullen and Rockart lay down an interviewing technique for eliciting CSFs.

Our interest is limited to obtaining the CSF of a manager and not in the techniques adopted in their definition. The technique of [11] allows CSF definition to be carried out. Given already defined CSFs, interest here is in obtaining information for estimating CSF satisfaction. Therefore, we need to define an elicitation technique for getting hold of this information.

Our use of CSF for information elicitation has two main benefits as follows:

1. It is relevant to manager concerns. Therefore, there is likely to be strong involvement of the manager in the requirements engineering task.
2. Since there are only a few CSFs for a manager, the DWRE task is manageable.

3.2.2   Ends Achievement

Ends achievement can be considered in two different ways, depending upon the way one conceptualizes the notion of Ends. These are as follows:

(1) An End is a statement about what is to be achieved, a goal. In this view, one can do Ends analysis by asking which Ends contribute to the achievement of which other Ends. Notice that an End is different from a CSF in that the latter is a work area where success is critical whereas End is that which is to be achieved.

(2) An End is the result achieved by performing a task or is the intended result of a decision. Therefore, unlike view (1) above, interest is not in determining which End achieves which given End. Rather, interest is in determining the information needed to ensure the effectiveness of the End. In other words, Ends analysis here is the identification of the needed information. We refer to it as **ENDSI** elicitation.

Notice the difference between the notion of a CSF and this view of Ends. Whereas a CSF is about success in a work area, an End is the expected result of a decision. A CSF is at a more "macro" level, whereas an End is relatively more focused and is at a "micro" level.

In our context, "Ends" refers to the result achieved by a decision. Therefore, requirements engineering is focussed on determining the information for the effectiveness of the result. The manager considers only those decisions that contribute positively to Ends effectiveness.

As for CSF above, we see that this ensures that the Ends effectiveness technique is close to the manager's view of a business and that it directly relates to decisions for promoting Ends effectiveness. This ensures continued manager interest in the requirements engineering task.

3.2.3   Means Efficiency

A means is of as much interest in the business world as are the notions of Ends and CSF. A means is an instrument for achieving an End and interest lies in determining the efficiency of the deployed means. Thus, we need a technique for determining means efficiency, thereby identifying information for evaluating the efficiency of the means. We refer to the technique for obtaining this information about means as **MEANSI** elicitation.

Just as for the Ends achievement technique, the means efficiency technique is close to the manager's view of the business. Since it directly relates to an important concern of managers, it ensures relatively high manager involvement in the requirements elicitation task.

3.2.4   Feedback Analysis

Sterman [13] has shown that feedback plays an important role in the area of dynamic decision-making. The business environment is changed by a decision. As a result, the conditions of choice get changed and these eventually feed back into the decision. A feedback cycle is formed. For example, let a manager take a decision to increase production. This changes the price, profits, and demand of goods. Consequently, there is an effect on the labor and materials market of the business. Additionally, customers may also react to the changed environment. All these affect future production decisions.

We interpret this feedback loop in terms of information. The manager needs information about each element (price, profit, etc.) in the feedback loop so as to make future production decisions.

3.2.5   Summary

To summarize, we propose to work with four major driving forces of a manager. We have identified these as (i) the manager must be "successful", (ii) the results delivered must be "effective", (iii) the manager must be efficient, and (iv) the manager must adapt and respond to the changing business environment.

A manager shall be motivated to **take those decisions that result in maximization of the achievement parameters**. To support this task, the data warehouse should keep information to help the manager in estimating the extent to which the achievement parameters are met.

Further, we consider it important to view our four techniques as a suite of elicitation techniques. Each technique takes a different perspective from the other and, in doing so, it views the information relevant to a decision from a different point of view. Consequently, the possibility of missing out on some information of relevance is reduced. This contributes to discovering more complete information.

3.3 Requirements Consolidation

We have seen that as the complexity of systems increases, incremental, iterative development starts becoming the preferred development strategy. It is no longer acceptable for requirements engineers to produce a requirements specification of the system to-be. Rather, we need to produce requirements granules corresponding to the granularity of the DW fragment. Each requirements granule leads to a DW fragment being developed. In other words, requirements granules for the increment at hand need to be produced.

Multitudes of requirements granules result in multitudes of DW fragments and when viewed from the perspective of the entire enterprise, this leads to inefficiencies and inconsistencies. Consolidation into a single physical data warehouse removes these difficulties and provides a better enterprise-wide data warehousing solution.

We have seen that the question of which DW fragments are to be developed and in what order is to be answered when doing strategic alignment. However, there is also the technological question of when and how consolidation is to be done. The current approach to answer this question is "detect and fix", according to which consolidation is done when operational DW fragments show unacceptable levels of inconsistency or inefficiency. This implies that

(a) Consolidation is not an integral part of the data warehouse development process. It is an add-on and is invoked as and when needed.
(b) We wait for a near breakdown of service to occur before fixing the problem. Necessarily, therefore, there shall be high dissatisfaction in the user community before we will even begin to address the problem. Further, since there shall be nontrivial lead time before the problem gets fixed, the period of dissatisfaction will be prolonged.
(c) There is considerable waste of effort. Existing designs and implementations must be discarded and a new integrated data warehouse must be built.
(d) If multiple existing DW fragments need to be consolidated, then the consolidation process shall be a one-shot process requiring large resources and time.

The question then is as to how we can obviate the foregoing difficulties.

The approach to consolidation in this book is driven by our desire to reduce the period of dissatisfaction of the user community. The principal means of doing this is to make the consolidation process an integral part of the incremental and iterative data warehouse development process. This implies that whenever a DW fragment is developed then it is consolidated with an existing DW fragment. In other words, the requirements granule of the existing DW fragment is compared with the requirements granule of the one to be developed. There are two possibilities

(1) Related DW fragments. The requirements granules contain common information that are conformed and a single requirements granule reflecting this conformity is developed. This granule then yields a consolidated DW fragment.
(2) Unrelated DW fragments. There is no common information between the two requirements granules. Therefore, we get two independent DW fragment requirements granules that yield two unrelated DW fragments.

Possibility (1) of related DW fragments implies that the consolidated DW fragment can be put on a common platform and has an integrated logical data model. In other words, we can do centralized consolidation described in Chap. 2. Possibility (2) means that we can put the DW fragments on the same common platform but we have two separate logical data models. There are cost savings due to the single platform and, in any case, inconsistencies do not occur since the DW fragments are unrelated.

To see how our approach works, let us assume that there are N existing DW fragments and K DW fragments are to be developed. Since, in our approach, requirements granules of the N DW fragments have already been compared, the only reason for these N to exist is that they are unrelated to one another. When comparing requirements granules, whereas there is no need to compare the requirements granules of these N with each other, requirement granules of the K DW fragments must be compared with one another and also with those of the N existing DW fragments so as to determine any related marts. Consider the possible strategies for comparing requirements granule as follows:

(a) Treat $N + K$ as a pool of DW fragments. Since comparison of requirements granules is to be done pair-wise, we get a total of $^{(N+K)}C_2$ combinations to compare. That is

$$\text{Number of combinations} = {}^{(N+K)}C_2 = ((N+K) * (N+K-1))/2$$

This strategy allows the possibility of comparing requirements granules of the N DW fragments with one another. Clearly, this is a waste.
(b) Treat N and K as separate. Now, we have to compare the requirements granules of K DW fragments with each other, yielding $^{K}C_2$ comparisons. Also, we can compare the K DW fragments with each of the N yielding $N * K$ comparisons. Consequently, we now get

$$\text{Number of combinations} = {}^{K}C_2 + N * K = (K * (K-1))/2 + N * K$$

This removes the problem with strategy (a) since there is no common pool of $(N + K)$ requirements granules. However, this strategy does not take into account that as a result of $^{K}C_2$ comparisons, some related DW fragments could have been identified. Therefore, the number of DW fragments to be compared with N is less than K.

(c) As in (b), we get $^{K}C_2$ comparisons. As a result, it is possible that some comparisons may result in combined requirements granules and some may not. We therefore get L requirements granules, $L \leq K$. Then, we need to compare these L with N thereby yielding

$$\text{Number of combinations} = {}^{K}C_2 + L * K = (K * (K - 1))/2 + L * N$$

It can be seen that all the three cases yield polynomial time complexity for the expression of the total number of comparisons to be made. At low values of N and K, doing the comparison may be even be possible but as these values rise, the problem starts to get out of hand. In other words, for large values of N and K, it is worthwhile to consider the "consolidate by redesign" approach to consolidation. However, for low values of N and K, we can still consider the incremental and iterative approach to consolidation.

We can convert our polynomial time complexity problem into a linear problem by making K = 1 and applying it to the expression in (c) above. As a consequence, L becomes equal to 1 since one DW fragment has to be built. Therefore, we get

$$\text{Number of combinations} = N$$

In other words, the requirements granule of the DW fragment to be built is compared with the N requirements granules of existing DW fragments. It is possible that the requirements granules of some $M \leq N$ DW fragments can be merged with the one being created. The expression for the number of DW fragments obtained is

$$\text{Number of DW fragments} = (N - M) + 1$$

If there are no matching requirements granules, then M = 0 and we get (N + 1) DW fragments since the new one is unrelated to any of the existing ones. On the other hand, if M = N, that is all the DW fragments match with the new one, then all can be combined in one logical data model and we get exactly one DW fragment.

However, enforcing that K = 1, while making our problem easier to handle, imposes a constraint on the number of new DW fragments that can be concurrently developed. That is, we sacrifice parallel DW fragment development and need to do it one at a time. To be sure, the delay in taking up the next DW fragment is till the time the comparison is over. Once the requirements granules are matched and the requirements granule of the new DW fragment is ready, then the next DW fragment for development can be taken up.

Our development process is shown in Fig. 3.6. In this process, the requirements engineering stage is in two parts. First, the requirements granule, RG, of the DW fragment to-be is developed. Thereafter, comparison with requirements granules of existing DW fragments, DWF_i (i between 1 and n) in the figure, is done. This results in the requirements granules of the (N − M) + 1 DW fragments as discussed earlier. The logical data models of the N − M DW fragments are not changed, whereas the M + 1 DW fragments get consolidated into a single logical data model.

As shown in Chap. 2, there are only two techniques for DW fragment consolidation, namely, DW fragment redesign and merge with primary. Adopting the former violates the incremental and iterative development principle that, as stated above, is our preferred approach. Thus, we are left with merge with primary as the alternative.

Our consolidation process does pair-wise consolidation as shown in Fig. 3.7. Let the organization start to build its first DW fragment, DWF_1, with requirements granule RG_1. This is shown by the dashed line between DWF_1 and RG_1 in the figure. There is no previous backlog of fragments and so RG_1 can be directly taken into development. When the organization starts on the second DW fragment $DWF2$, then an attempt is made to integrate its requirements specification, RG_2 with RG_1. If these are disjoint, then we get two separate DW fragments in the organization. If, however, these have commonalities, then we get the integrated requirements specification, RG_3, that is then taken through the development life cycle to yield a physically and logically unified data warehouse fragment, DFW_2. For the third DW fragment, we either have two disjoint DW fragments or a consolidated one. In either case, the requirements of the new DW fragment are matched with those of the existing ones, to, as before, either add to the backlog of disjoint DW fragments or do further consolidation. This process continues for each DW fragment to be developed. The figure shows the case where consolidation of RG_3 with the new requirements granule RG_4 can be performed.

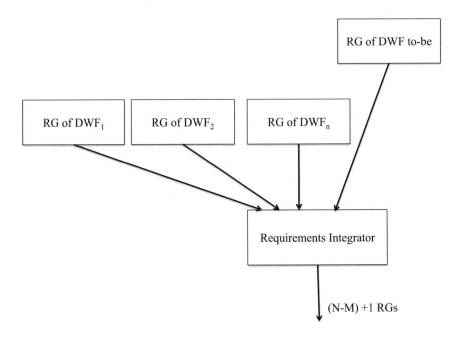

Fig. 3.6 Integrating requirements

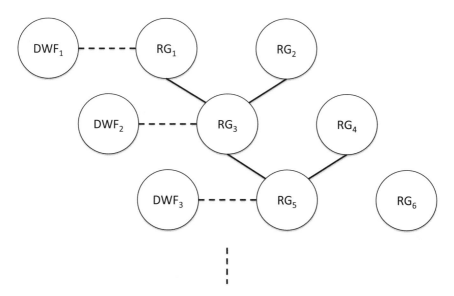

Fig. 3.7 Pair-wise integration of requirement fragments

It can be seen that the underlying development principle of the process model is to "build by integrating". That is, rather than wait for inconsistency and cost issues to arise and then treat consolidation as a separate process to be carried out, our approach is to check out the possibility of integration during the requirements engineering process itself. This forces a comprehensive look at the DW fragments being developed in the organization by the IT department. The chances of having multiple platforms therefore reduce. Additionally, DW fragment proliferation is minimized since whatever can be integrated is in fact consolidated upfront in the requirements engineering stage.

Additionally, the cost of developing new fragments that can be integrated with others is minimized. We can see this by considering RG_2 in Fig. 3.7. Under the traditional approach, no effort would be made to match it against RG_1. The requirements in RG_2 would result in an implemented data mart. However, the development effort would be wasted since the design and implementation would be discarded at the time integration, with RG_1, eventually occurs. In the "build by integration" approach, this effort would not be put in, as the possibility of integration is spotted during requirements engineering. However, if there is no commonality between RG_1 and RG_2, then effort would be put in development of RG_2 and similar costs as with the traditional approach would be incurred.

This suggests that the "build by integration" approach provides best results when the DW fragments that have common information are taken up for development in the organization. These results in

(a) Minimization of wasted development effort.
(b) Minimization of platform and process costs.
(c) Minimization of inconsistency problems.

If, however, DW fragments are disjoint, then only benefits as in (b) and (c) accrue.

It follows that this aspect should be taken into account when strategically aligning the data warehouse project to the organization. The benefits that accrue from a DW fragment in the BI perspective would need to be balanced with the expenses involved in the technical perspective, namely, wasted development effort, platform, and process costs, as well as cost of inconsistency problems. Convergence between the BI and technical perspectives occurs when the technical expenses are minimized by selecting closely related DW fragments.

The main features and advantages of the "build by integration" approach are as follows:

- It attempts to reach a consolidation of DW fragments as early as possible. Proliferation only occurs when the pair-wise integration technique fails to identify any commonality.
- It resembles the merge with primary approach. However, it is the new DW fragment rather than an existing DW fragment that drives integration.
- It differs from the merge with primary approach in doing integration in the requirements stage itself.
- Data inconsistency problems just do not arise. Thus, it is a preventive approach rather than a detection and correction approach.
- By limiting proliferation and always looking for consolidation, our approach minimizes costs associated with hosting multiple marts.

3.4 Conclusion

The focus on decisions highlights the decision-making that a data warehouse supports. Since information relevant to the decisions to be supported is required, the information elicitation process is driven by such decisions. This provides a very basic form of guidance in the elicitation task namely, look for exactly that information which is relevant to decisions. It also reduces the fuzziness associated with identifying information required to carry out "analysis" since the nature of the analysis is not specifically articulated.

Managers/decision-makers want to maximize their achievements and they shall take decisions that meet this objective. Managerial interest would be in building DW fragments for such decisions. The information elicitation process should then support this by obtaining information that helps in estimating the extent of manager achievement. The four aspects to be covered by the process are CSFI, MEANSI, ENDSI, and outcome feedback, respectively.

Finally, we saw the problem of proliferation of DW fragments and the build-by-integration approach. We argued against building requirements specifications for subject-oriented data marts. Instead, we need to build requirements granules for decisions. As new decisions and associated requirement granules are taken up, requirements integration should be attempted. The most beneficial situation is when consolidation with existing DW fragments occurs. The next best situation is when DW fragments are disjoint but even this is better than the current practice in data mart integration because of the determination that inconsistency just cannot occur and also because of the increased possibility of a single enterprise-wide platform.

In the rest of this book, we consider the methods, tools, and techniques that address the issues raised here.

References

1. "Wikipedia, The free encyclopedia", http://en.wikipedia.org/wiki/Decision.
2. Turban, E., Aronson Jay, E. (1998, January). *Decision support systems and intelligent systems* (5th ed.). Prentice Hall.
3. Makarov, I. M., Vinogradskaya, M. T., Rubchinsky, A. A., & Sokolov, V. B. (1987). *The theory of choice and decision making*. Moscow: Mir Publishers.
4. Simon, H. A. (1977). *The new science of management decision*. Englewood Cliffs, NJ: Prentice Hall.
5. Baker, D., Bridges, D., Hunter, R., Johnson, G., Krupa, J., Murphy, J., Sorenson, K. (2001). *Guidebook to decision-making methods*. Developed for the Department of Energy. http://emi-web.inel.gov/Nissmg/Guidebook_2002.pdf.
6. Saaty, T. L. (1980). *The analytic hierarchy process*. NY: McGraw Hil.
7. Keeney, R. L., & Raiffa, H. (1993). *Decisions with multiple objectives: Preferences and value trade-offs*. Cambridge University Press.
8. Keeney, R. L. (1999). Foundations for making smart decisions. *IIE Solutions, 31*(5), 24–30.
9. Fuller, R., & Carlsson, C. (1996). Fuzzy multiple criteria decision making: Recent developments. *Fuzzy Sets and Systems, 78,* 139–153.
10. Moisiadis, F. (2005). *A framework for prioritizing use case*. Australia: Joint Research Centre for Advanced Systems Engineering.
11. Bullen, C. V., Rockart, J. F. (1981). A primer of critical success factors. CISR No. 69 Sloan WP No. 1220-81 Center for Information Systems Research, Sloan School of Management Massachusetts Institute of Technology, 1981.
12. Wetherbe, J. C., Davis, G. B. (1983). Developing a long-range information architecture. In: *Proceedings of AFIPS*, pp. 261–269.
13. Sterman, J. D. (1989). Modeling managerial behaviour: Misperceptions of feedback in a dynamic decision making experiment. *Management Science, 35*(3), 321–339.

Chapter 4
Discovering Decisions

Given the central role that the decision plays, the critical step in developing a DW fragment is that of establishing the decision or collection of decisions that the fragment shall support. Since the notion of a DW fragment is neutral to the nature of decision that it supports, we need to define the different kinds of decisions that there can be, where they originate from, and how they can be defined.

We have already seen that there are three levels of decisions in a business, for formulating policies, policy enforcement rules, and also operational decisions. The interesting issue now is that of determining these decisions. That is, support for the task of obtaining decisions is to be provided.

In Sect. 4.1, we address the issue of formulating policies of an enterprise. There is wide spread recognition that the task of policy formulation is a complex one. In order to do this, we consider the meaning of the term, policy. Thereafter, we represent policies in a formalism based on the first-order predicate logic. We show that a statement of this logic, therefore a policy, can be represented as a hierarchy. The nodes of this hierarchy are components of the policy. Lastly, we associate the possibility of selecting, rejecting, or modifying any node of the hierarchy. This yields the set of decisions for formulating enterprise policies.

The issue of formulating policy enforcement rules is taken up in Sect. 4.2. Since these rules are for policy enforcement, it is necessary that the policy corresponding to the rule is already formulated. A representation system for policy enforcement rules is presented and a collection of rules and guidelines is developed to obtain policy enforcement rules from policies. The developed rules are associated with operators to select, reject, and modify them. This yields the set of decisions using which enforcement rules of the enterprise are formulated.

Finally, we consider operational decision-making in Sect. 4.3. Operational decision-making first involves examining the policy enforcement rules applicable to the situation at hand to select the most appropriate one. In Sect. 4.3, the structure of

© Springer Nature Singapore Pte Ltd. 2018
N. Prakash and D. Prakash, *Data Warehouse Requirements Engineering*,
https://doi.org/10.1007/978-981-10-7019-8_4

the action suggested by the rule is presented. This is an AND/OR hierarchy. The OR branches in this hierarchy define alternatives and constitute a choice set from which selection of the most appropriate branch is made. Thus, we have decisions of the operational level of an enterprise.

4.1   Deciding Enterprise Policies

Policy formulation is done in a number of contexts, in government/public policy formulation [1], in the corporate/business world [2], in specific areas like manufacturing [3], and accounting [4]. The stakeholders are also varied and comprise [1, 5] general public, opinion makers, service providers, service users, activists, etc. Some other factors going into policy formulation are

- The role of other corporates [6] in the formulation of policy by a business house;
- Dependence [3] on other related policies;
- The role of consensus building [5]; and
- The strategy (information, financial incentive, and constituency building), level of participation (individual, collective), and action (transactional and relational) to be adopted [2].

Thus, it can be easily seen that policy formulation is a many-facetted and complex task.

The Oxford advanced learner's dictionary defines a policy in the following three ways:

1. "A plan of action agreed or chosen by a political party, a business, etc.";
2. "A principal that you believe in that influences how you behave; a way in which you usually behave"; and
3. "A written statement of a contract of insurance".

In our context, we are interested in 1 and 2 above.

Blakemore [7] defines policy as "aims or goals or statements of what ought to happen." According to [8], policies "are directly derived from corporate goals and thus embody aspects of strategic business management." Anderson [9] says "A policy is typically described as a principle or rule to guide decisions and achieve rational outcome(s)". OMG's SBVR [10] considers a policy to be an "element of governance that *is not directly enforceable* whose purpose is to guide an enterprise."

The foregoing definitions emphasize that policies are the touchstone against which the appropriateness of courses of actions/decisions/behavior is determined. We **consider a policy as a specification of the desired properties of an organization**. These properties may be defined by regulatory bodies, organizations that lay down standards, and so on.

Now, consider an organization with a set of policies P. For a newly conceived organization, this set may be empty and the organization will have to define its policies. On the other hand, for existing organizations the set P consists of a number of legacy policies. Also, in an organization policies evolve. This may be due to changes in (a) operational realities or (b) business realities, for example, business environment or regulations, etc. may change. In either case, heads of organizations consult policies specified by regulators as well as examine best practices of other similar businesses to determine their own policies. This raises the issue of supporting decision-making for deciding which policies to adopt.

A policy [11] governs strategies/tactics. Strategies/tactics are the instruments available in organizations to obtain the desired results. Results may be expressed in different ways, goals, objectives, targets, etc. Therefore, starting point for developing policy data warehouse can be goals of the organization. However, adopting **goal-orientated** DWRE makes the process very heavy. This is because the following steps would have to be performed so as to determine:

A. goals,
B. strategies/tactics,
C. policies for strategies/tactics,
D. information relevant to each policy, and lastly,
E. the multidimensional structure.

Another approach is to explore a rich source of already available policies. These sources are as follows:

- Regulatory bodies and other organizations charged with lying down norms and standards. Examples of such norms are hygiene norms for restaurants; health norms for hospitals and nursing homes; accreditation standards for educational institutions, etc.
- Other "best practice" organizations of the same domain; and
- An organizations' own legacy policies.

Using these policies as a starting point makes the requirements engineering task relatively lighter. This makes possible an approach to requirements engineering that can reuse existing norms, standards, and policies. Each policy that is available can be accepted/selected, or modified to a different but similar one, or rejected. The entire process involves the following steps:

A. Represent "given" policies,
B. Generate a structural hierarchy based on the representation, and
C. Associate a choice set that will be lead to either selecting or modifying or rejecting the policy. This yields the set of decisions for policy formulation.

Let us discuss each of the steps of the policy reuse-based approach.

4.1.1 *Representing Policies*

Policies are declarations and so a declarative form of representation is considered most appropriate for policies. Consider two forms of declarations, natural language, and logic. Natural language is relatively free flowing and does not have the formally defined structure of logic. As is well known, a statement in a logic system is a well-defined formula that is built over simpler well-defined formulae. Also, the Business Rules Manifesto says "expressions in logic are fundamental to represent business rules as business people see them." Just as SBVR [10] for representing policies, a natural language capacity can be developed with its semantics based on the first-order logic.

This structuring offers an advantage in policy formulation since each component can be examined and its appropriateness considered. The first-order representation of policies with certain extensions for representing sets of values as variables of the logic is as follows:

Variables are of two kinds, those that denote:

> A single value, SV, and
>
> A set of values, CV.

A *simple term, ST*, can either be a

> constant,
>
> an SV,
>
> or an n-adic function symbol applied to n SVs.

A *collective term, CT*, is either

> a CV or
>
> an n - adic function symbol applied to n CVs.

An *atom* is an n-place predicate $P(x_1, x_2, ..., x_n)$ where any x_i is either ST or CT. There are standard predicates for the six relational operators named EQ (x, y), NEQ (x, y), GEQ (x, y), LEQ (x, y), GQ (x, y), and LQ (x, y).

The formulae of the logic are defined as follows:

- Every atom is a formula.
- If F1 and F2 are formulae, then F1 AND F2, F1 OR F2, and Not F1 are formulae.
- If F1 and F2 are formulae, then F1 $\rightarrow$ F2 is also a formula.
- If F1 is a formula, then $\exists$sF1 and $\forall$sF1 are formulae. Here, s is SV or CV.
- Parenthesis may be placed around formulae as needed.
- Nothing else is a formula.

The precedence while evaluating the formulae is as follows:

- Universal and existential quantifiers, $\forall$, $\exists$
- Logical AND, OR, NOT

Let us represent some policies in logic described above. Consider the following examples.

Policy 1: Every AYUSH hospital must operate an outpatients department, OPD.

$$\forall a[AyH(a) \rightarrow operate(a, OPD)]$$

where

AyH(a) says that a is AYUSH hospital and
operate (a, OPD) says that a must operate an OPD.

Policy 2: A semi-private ward has an area of 200 ft^2 and two beds.

$$\forall s \exists B[spw(s) \rightarrow EQ(count(B), 2) AND\ EQ(area(s), 200)]$$

where

spw(s) says that s is a semi-private ward,
EQ(s,c1) says that s is equal to c1, and
B is a set of beds.

4.1.2   Policies to Choice Sets

Using the well-formed formulae, a policy is expressed into its structural hierarchy. For this, the structure of the formulae is decomposed into two parts, the part on the left-hand side of the implication and the second part that is on the right-hand side of the implication. These parts can themselves be reduced into formulae and this decomposition ends when atoms are reached. This provides us a hierarchical structure for each policy. Figure 4.1 shows a policy P decomposed into formulae F1, F2, … Fn. Each of these is further decomposed and the process continues till the leaves of the hierarchy are reached. These leaves are the atoms of the policy.

Fig. 4.1 Structural hierarchy of a policy

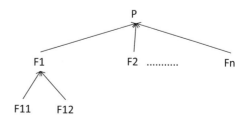

The algorithm used to generate this hierarchy is as follows.

Algorithm: To generate policy hierarchy tree for a given policy
Input: Policy in first order logic form
Output: Policy hierarchy
{

    addroot(formula, root) //add policy as root of the tree
    if formula contains quantifiers //(of the form $\forall$x or $\exists$x)
        $formula_Q$ = formula minus quantifiers extracted from formula
        addchild($formula_Q$, root) //add $formula_Q$ to root
    if $formula_Q$ contains implication '$\rightarrow$'
        $formula_L$ = formula on left side of implication
        $formula_R$ = formula on right side of implication
        PT_L= makept($formula_L$) //make a postfix tree, makept, from $formula_L$
        Attach_pt_as_child(PT_L, $formula_Q$) //attach the postfix tree, pt, to $formula_Q$
        PT_R = makept($formula_R$) //make postfix tree from $formula_R$
        Attach_pt_as_child(PT_R, $formula_Q$) //attach the postfix tree, pt, to $formula_Q$

}

The algorithm starts with the full statement of the policy as the root. Subsequently, it examines the root for the presence of quantifiers and removes them giving us the child node which has the root node as it's parent node. Subsequent levels are added by splitting this node into two formulae, one on the right side of the implication and the other on the left side. Thereafter, postfix trees are built for both the sides. These subtrees are then attached to their respective parent nodes giving us the policy hierarchy. The leaves of the final tree are atoms.

As an example, take Policy 1, the policy "Every doctor must have a post graduate degree".

$$\forall x[doc(x) \rightarrow degree(x, MD)]$$

Figure 4.2 shows the process of developing a policy hierarchy.

Consider the Policy 2. Figure 4.3 shows the application of the policy hierarchy algorithm.

Now, consider choice set construction. It is possible to select, modify, or reject an atom. Thus, we get the choice set {select, modify, reject} associated with all atoms. Now, we move one level above the leaf level. Here, atoms are connected together using AND, OR, NOT; implication ($\rightarrow$); and by placing parenthesis. At this level, again we accept, reject, or modify formulae. In fact, at each level of the hierarchy it is possible to associate the choice set {select, reject, modify}. And this eventually results in the acceptance, rejection, or modification of the policy P. Applying choice sets to the policy hierarchy shown in Fig. 4.2, we get Fig. 4.4a.

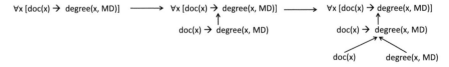

Fig. 4.2 Policy hierarchy for "Every doctor must have a post graduate degree"

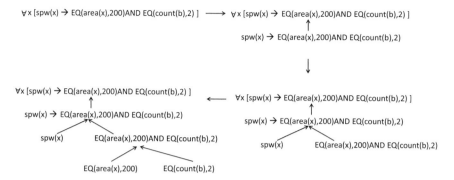

Fig. 4.3 A complex policy

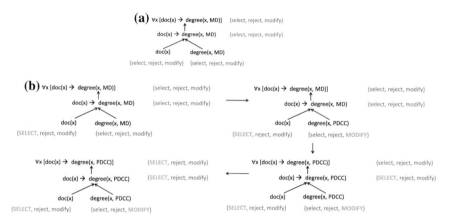

Fig. 4.4 a Hierarchy for "Every doctor must have a postgraduate Degree". **b** The process of adopting a policy

It can thus be seen that "given" policies are represented using first-order logic and subsequently converted to a policy hierarchy. Choice sets {select node, modify node, reject node} are associated with each node of the hierarchy.

Reusing Policies

Now the question is how these policy hierarchies are used by any organization to formulate its own policies. First, the organization constructs the policy hierarchy. Then starting from the leftmost leaf, decision-makers move up the tree in a bottom-up manner. As each node is processed, an alternative from the choice set {select, modify, reject} is picked. The tree is fully processed once the root node has been selected, modified, or rejected. The algorithm is shown below.

Repeat until root of hierarchy

(1) Traverse policy hierarchy tree in bottom-up left right manner;
(2) For each node visited, consult the data warehouse; and
(3) From choice set {select node, modify node, reject node}, pick alternative.

In order to decide on an alternative from the choice set, the decision-maker will require information. If relevant information is present in the data warehouse, then this information can be consulted and an alternative from this choice set can be selected so as to formulate the organizational policy.

Using the policy hierarchy shown in Fig. 4.4a, let us first describe steps (1) and (3). It is assumed here that step (2) is performed every time after step (1) is performed.

A choice set using {select, modify, reject} is constructed for (a) the two atoms doc(x) and degree(x, MD) respectively, (b) the next hierarchical level formula, and (c) the full policy. Selection of doc(x) says that in our new policy this atom is retained. Its rejection means that the policy is to be reframed and possibly a new one formulated. Its modification implies the modification of the predicate doc(x) and essentially results in a creation of a new policy. Assume that doc(x) is selected. The left topmost corner of Fig. 4.4b shows that the decision SELECT (marked in orange) is taken and so doc(x) is selected.

Now consider the second atom. Its selection means that the atom is retained; rejection means that possibly a new policy is to be formulated; modification may mean that the qualification required may be PDCC. Assume that this modification is to be done. The choice "Modify" will be selected and therefore, marked with orange in the figure and the value of the node will be changed. The figure also shows the selection of the implication at the next level and the selection of the universal quantifier at the root. Again, selection, modification, or rejection is possible. The selection of the root node means that the entire policy has been selected. One way of modifying is the replacement of the universal quantifier with the existential quantifier. Rejection at the root level means that we are rejecting the binding of the variable to a quantifier. This means that the entire policy is in fact rejected.

To conclude, the well-defined formulae of the first-order logic makes it possible to examine each sub-formula recursively in order to decide whether to select, reject, or modify as discussed above. By making an appropriate choice, we can formulate modified policies, reject existing policies, or create new policies.

Such a policy hierarchy is constructed for each policy that may be defined by a regulatory body, standardization body, or that may be available as best practice of another organization or as a legacy policy of an organization.

4.2   Deciding Policy Enforcement Rules

Once policies have been formulated, the next problem is that of formulating policy enforcement rules. When an action is performed in an organization, there are two possibilities. One, that this action does not violate any policy. Two, that this action violates a policy. Clearly, the latter situation needs to be handled so that there is policy compliance. Thus, interest here is in formulating rules that specify corrective actions to be taken.

Let us revisit the structure of policies, defined in Sect. 4.1.1. We can see that policies can have either simple or complex formulae. Complex formulae are those involving

- Conjunctions (AND) and disjunctions (OR) and
- n-adic functions.

Since a policy is of the form quantifier (IF Formula1 THEN Formula2), we obtain four kinds of business policies, as shown in Table 4.1, where S stands for simple and C for complex. These depend on the nature of Formula1 and Formula2.

A simple policy, SS policy, has both Formula1 and Formula2 as simple. Thus the policy, "Every doctor must have an M.D. degree" expressed as $\forall x[doc(x) \rightarrow degree(x, MD)]$, has no conjunction/disjunction or n-adic function on either LHS or its RHS and thus is a simple policy.

Row numbers two, three, and four of Table 4.1 have at least one formula as complex. The policy is of simple–complex (SC) type. Consider the policy, $\forall y \exists B \exists N [GB(y) \rightarrow ratio(count(N), count(B),1,8)]$. Since the right-hand side uses functions, it is complex. LHS is simple. This is an SC-type policy. Another example is $\forall x \exists b [S(x) \rightarrow LEQ(count(b),3) \text{ AND } GT(count(b),1)]$. The RHS contains both a function and AND conjunction. LHS is a simple formula making the policy of SC type.

Now, let us look at row three of Table 4.1. Here, the situation is reverse of that in row two. The LHS is complex but the RHS is simple and we have a CS policy. Consider the policy $\forall x[housekeeper(x) \text{ OR } nurse(x) \rightarrow Offer(x,PF)]$. LHS of the implication uses the conjunction and is thus complex. The RHS is simple making this policy CS-type policy.

The last row of Table 4.1 considers a CC policy as having complex formulae on both sides of the implication. The policy $\forall x \exists wtabSet \exists ftabSet [woodTable(x) \text{ OR } fibreTable(x) \rightarrow Sum(count(wtabSet), count(ftabSet),2)]$ has a conjunction OR on

Table 4.1 The types of policies

S. No.	Formula1	Formula2	Type of policy
1	S	S	Simple, SS
2	S	C	Complex, SC
3	C	C	Complex, CS
4	C	C	Complex, CC, subsumed in 2 and 3

the LHS of the implication and function count() on the RHS, both of which are complex. Thus, this policy is a complex–complex policy.

Consider the situation when in the general form of a policy, Quantifier(IF Formula1 THEN Formula2), Formula1 is true and Formula2 false. This indicates a policy is violated. Let there be an action A that causes Formula1 to be True. If Formula2 is True, then no violation has occurred. On the other hand, if Formula2 is False, then corrective action say B needs to be carried out so that Formula2 becomes True.

Let us assume now that another action A causes the Formula2 on the RHS to become False. This implies that either an action C must be performed to make Formula1 False or that the action A itself should be disallowed.

In the subsequent sections, we discuss (a) representation of policy enforcement rules and (b) elicitation of actions A, B, and C above.

4.2.1 Representing Enforcement Rules

Policy enforcement rules are a type of business rules. Business rules have been represented by either natural language-based approaches or logic-based approaches. Natural language representation has been used in [12, 13]. Leite and Leonardi [12] defines business rules expressed in natural language using specified patterns. Fu et al. [13] makes use of templates. A template consists of different kinds of expressions, for example, determiner and subject expressions. SBVR uses its own definition of Structured English for expressing business rules. A predicate logic-based Business Rules Language, BRL, was proposed by Fu et al. [13] but this has only a limited number of built-in predicates.

Logic-based representation expressed in the IF-THEN form has been used by Auechaikul and Vatanawood [14]. Two variants of this form have been proposed, IF-THEN-ELSE by Muehlen and Kamp [15] and WHEN-IF-DO by Rosca et al. [16].

We need to use the notion of an action in order to represent policy enforcement rules. There can be two kinds of actions:

- **Triggering**: This type of action triggers a policy violation. This action could on the Then side of the implication and cause the IF side to be false. It can also be on the IF side causing the Then side to be false. Action A above is a triggering action.
- **Correcting**: As stated once there is a policy violation, suitable corrective action has to be taken. Actions B and C above are correcting actions.

Since an activity fact type is absent in SBVR [10], we must explore a more direct way to represent triggering and correcting actions. Indeed, a representation in logic shall not yield a direct representation of triggers and actions which will need to be derived from the functions/predicates comprising well-formed formulas of the logic. Therefore, the WHEN part of a rule contains the triggering action; the condition to be checked when the triggering action has occurred in the IF part; and the THEN part contains correcting action to be taken. Therefore, a policy-enforcing rule is represented as

WHEN *triggering action* **IF** *condition* **THEN** *correcting action*

Notice the similarity of the policy enforcement rule with that of the notion of a trigger in SQL. A trigger [17] is a stored program; a pl/sql block structure that is fired when INSERT/UPDATE/DELETE operations are performed and certain conditions are satisfied. There are thus three components to a trigger, an event, a condition, and an action corresponding to the WHEN, IF, and THEN part, respectively.

In SQL, a trigger is seen as an executable component. However, a policy enforcement rule is a directive that governs/guides [11] a future course of action. Seeing this similarity with SQL, we use here the basic idea behind a range variable of SQL.

The remaining question is about the representation of an action. Actions, both triggering and correcting, are of the form **<verb> <range variable>**. To see this, let us first consider the notion of a range variable.

A range variable denotes an instance of a noun. Before using it, a range variable is declared using the form:

$$< range\ variable > \ = \ <noun > \ \ <range\ variable >$$

A noun can be simple or a noun–noun modification. A noun *Ayurvedic Hospital* built over two nouns Ayurvedic and Hospital is an example of the latter, where Ayurvedic is a noun that modifies Hospital. We will italicize range variables for easy identification.

As examples of declaration of range variables, consider

$$<OPD > \ <x >$$
$$<Ayurvedic\ Hospital > \ <y >$$

In the first example, OPD is a noun and x is its range variable. This says that x is an instance of OPD. Similarly, in the second example, y is an instance of Ayurvedic Hospital.

Now we can construct actions which, as mentioned above, are of the form <verb> <range variable>. Using the range variables x and y declared above, we can define actions, create *x* and operate *y,* respectively.

The policy enforcement rules from above now can be written as

WHEN <**verb** > <**range variable** > **IF condition THEN** <**verb** > <**range variable** >

4.2.2   Developing Choice Sets

In order for the requirements engineer to formulate PER for a policy P, s/he has to decide on the possible correcting actions for a triggering action. Let this be the set {corrAction1, corrAction2, corrAction3…}.

On examining this set closely, one finds that in fact with every action there is a choice the requirements engineer has to make, whether to select, modify, or reject the action. In other words, the choice set presented to the requirements engineer is

{**select** corrAction1, **modify** corrAction1, **reject** corrAction1, **select** corrAction2, **modify** corrAction2………}

The actions selected become part of the PER, rejected actions are not part of any PER, and the modified actions become part of the PER. For example, if corrAction1 and corrAction2 are selected and corrAction3 is rejected, then the requirements engineer arrives at two PER:

> WHEN trigAction1 IF violatingCondition THEN corrAction1
>
> WHEN trigAction1 IF violatingCondition THEN corrAction2

Note, the same action can be a correcting action for more than one kind of triggering action. Also, a triggering action in one PER can be a correcting action in another PER and vice versa.

In order to elicit the required action, the following two macro-guidelines are used. This applies to all the four types of policies, SS, SC, CS, and CC.

- **Guideline I**: The requirements engineer defines triggering actions to make LHS true. Since policies are violated when the RHS becomes false, correcting actions are elicited to make **RHS true**.
- **Guideline II**: The requirements engineer defines triggering actions to make RHS false. Since a policy is violated, its left-hand side becomes true. Correcting actions are elicited to make the **LHS false**.

Once the actions have been elicited, the policy enforcement rule is formulated by filling the "WHEN-IF-THEN" form with the triggering and connecting actions.

Let us look at the application of the guidelines for the four kinds of policies.

SS-Type Policy

Consider the following policy:
Example I: Every Ayurvedic hospital must operate an outpatients department.

$$\forall a[ayH(a) \rightarrow operate(a, OPD)]$$

Since actions are of the form <verb> <range variable>, we start by defining range variables as follows:

$$<\text{Ayurvedic hospital}> \quad <h>$$
$$<\text{OPD}> \quad <o>$$

Applying the two guidelines, we get the following:

Applying Guideline I

The requirements engineer defines triggering actions to make the LHS, ayH(x) true. Let this action be "create Ayurvedic hospital". By guideline I above, correcting actions need to be elicited to make RHS, operate(x, OPD) true. Let the elicited actions be

(a) Start OPD,
(b) construct OPD, and
(c) reuse OPD.

The policy enforcement rules are as follows:

- WHEN create h IF !operate(h, o) THEN start o
- WHEN create h IF !operate (h, o) THEN construct o
- WHEN create h IF !operate (h, o) THEN reuse o

Notice "create h" has created as the verb and "h" as range variable.

Applying Guideline II

Let the triggering action be "stop OPD" which makes the RHS false. The requirements engineer elicits corrective actions to make the LHS false. Let these be

(a) stop functioning as an Ayurvedic hospital and
(b) re-designate hospital.

Thus, the policy enforcement rules obtained are

- WHEN stop o IF ayH (h) THEN stop h
- WHEN stop o IF ayH (h) THEN re-designate h

SC-Type Policy

Recall, a complex SC-type policy has LHS as simple and RHS as complex. Since LHS is simple, actions for LHS are elicited in the same way as with simple policy types described above. Elicitation strategies are formulated for complex predicate (formula) on the RHS.

Unlike general-purpose languages, special-purpose languages do not have full expressive power [15]. Consequently, recourse to standard predicates is taken as seen in [15] where predefined standard predicates are defined. These standard predicates can be connected using AND/OR operators.

For complex predicates here, standard predicates along with the elicitation strategy are defined as shown in Table 4.2. Consider row 1 that defines standard predicate EQ(Function(x),c). This is complex due to function Function(x). If Function(x) evaluates to a value less than constant c, then correcting action must increase the value of the function so that it satisfies the predicate. If, however, its value is greater than constant c, its value must be decreased by the correcting action. This approach applies to all rows of the table.

Let us now consider an example.

Example I: Each private room must have an area of 200 ft^2 expressed as

$$\forall x[\text{pvtR}(x) \rightarrow \text{EQ}(\text{area}(x), 200)]$$

Table 4.2 Elicitation strategies for standard complex RHS predicates

S. No.	Standard complex RHS Predicate	Elicitation Strategy *to make RHS True*
1	EQ(Function(x),c)	If Function(x) is less than c then elicit action to increase Function(x) If Function(x) is greater than c then elicit action to reduce Function(x)
2	LEQ(Function(x),c)	If Function(x) is greater than c then elicit action to reduce Function(x)
3	LT(Function(x),c)	If Function(x) is equal to c then elicit action to reduce Function(x) If Function(x) is greater than c then elicit action to reduce Function(x)
4	GT(Function(x),c)	If Function(x) is less than c then elicit action to increase Function(x) If Function(x) is equal to c then elicit action to increase Function(x)
5	GEQ(Function(x),c)	If Function(x) is less than c then elicit action to increase Function(x)
6	NEQ(Function(x),c)	If Function(x) is equal to c then elicit action to increase Function(x) or elicit action to reduce Function(x)
7	Ratio(Function1(x), Function2(y),c1,c2)	If Function1(x)/Function2(y) less than c1/c2 then elicit action to increase Function1(x) or elicit action to reduce Function2(y) If Function1(x)/Function2(y) greater than c1/c2 then elicit action to increase Function2(y) or elicit action to reduce Function1(x)
8	Percent(Function1(x), Function2(y),c)	If Function1(x)/Function2(y) is not equal to c then elicit action to increase Function1(x)/Function2(y) or elicit action to reduce Function1(x)/Function2(y)
9	Sum(Function1(x), Function2(y),c)	If Function1(x)+Function2(y) is less than c then elicit action to increase Function1(x) or increase Function2(y) If Function1(x)+Function2(y) is greater than c then elicit action to reduce Function2(y) or reduce Function1(x)

As before, the first step is to define range variables:

$$<\text{Private Room}> \quad <pr>$$

Applying Guideline I

Let the requirement engineer elicit triggering action "create private room". This makes LHS true. At this moment, RHS is false and therefore the first row of Table 4.2 is applied. The elicitation strategy suggested is to elicit correcting action to

1. Increase the value of area(x). The elicited actions are

   (a) Rebuild private room and
   (b) Expand private room.

2. Reduce the value of area(x). The elicited action is

   (a) Partition private room.

Using the elicited triggering and correcting actions, the following rules are obtained:

- WHEN create *pr* IF LT(area(*pr*),200) THEN Rebuild *pr*
- WHEN create *pr*, IF LT(area(*pr*),200) THEN Expand *pr*
- WHEN create *pr*, IF GT(area(*pr*),200) THEN Partition *pr*

Applying Guideline II

Suppose triggering action "partition room" causes the available area of a room to reduce. This makes RHS false. A correcting action needs to be elicited to make LHS false. Notice that LHS is a simple formula and so actions can be elicited as with SS type of policy. Assume that the elicited correcting action is "relocate private room".

The policy enforcement rule obtained is

- WHEN partition *pr* IF !EQ(area(*pr*),200) THEN relocate *pr*

Example II: Consider the following example:

$$\forall x \exists b [S(x) \rightarrow LEQ(\text{count}(b), 3) \text{ AND } GT(\text{count}(b), 1)]$$

Range variables are

$$<\text{Semi-private ward}> \quad <spw>$$
$$<\text{bed}> \quad <b>$$

Table 4.3 Elicitation strategy for LEQ and GT predicates

Standard LEQ RHS predicate	Standard GT RHS predicate
True	True
True	False: elicit action to increase Function(x)
False: elicit action to reduce Function(x)	False: elicit action to increase Function(x)
False: elicit action to reduce Function(x)	True

Applying Guideline I

Let the triggering action be "create spw". Notice, correcting actions will be formed by a combination of actions of LEQ and GT. Table 4.3 suggests four possibilities.

When a new semi-private ward is created, then the number of beds is zero and so function count(b) gives value zero. This makes LEQ predicate to evaluate to true and GT predicate to be false. As suggested by the second row of Table 4.3, elicitation strategy to make GT to be true has to be explored to make the entire RHS true. Thus, applying fourth row of Table 4.2 the elicited actions may be

(a) Purchase bed and
(b) Transfer bed.

So the policy enforcement rules are

- WHEN create *spw* IF !GT(count(b),1) THEN Purchase b
- WHEN create *spw* IF !GT(count(b),1) THEN Transfer b

Applying Guideline II

Now, the removal of a bed from the ward may result in a bedless ward, thereby violating GT(count(b),1). Correcting actions to make LHS false must be obtained. Let this be "Relocate semi-private ward".

The policy enforcement rule obtained is

- WHEN remove b IF !(GT(count(b),1)) THEN Relocate *spw*

Complex CS-Type Policy

For a CS policy, LHS is complex while RHS is simple. The elicitation strategy used for RHS in the same as that of simple policy types. For complex predicate on the LHS, new elicitation strategies are formulated. Again, a set of standard predicates are used. Table 4.4 gives the standard LHS predicates along with the elicitation strategy.

Table 4.4 Elicitation strategies for given LHS predicate

S. No.	Standard complex LHS predicate	Elicitation strategy *to make LHS True*
1	EQ(Function(x),c)	If Function(x) is equal to c then elicit action to make RHS true
2	LEQ(Function(x),c)	If Function(x) is less than or equal to c then elicit action to make RHS true
3	LT(Function(x),c)	If Function(x) is less than c then elicit action to make RHS true
4	GT(Function(x),c)	If Function(x) is greater than c then elicit action to make RHS true
5	GEQ(Function(x),c)	If Function(x) is greater than or equal to c then elicit action to make RHS true
6	NEQ(Function(x),c)	If Function(x) is not equal to c then elicit action to make RHS true
7	Ratio(Function1(x), Function2(y), c1, c2)	If Function1(x)/Function2(y) is equal to c1/c2 then elicit action to make RHS true
8	Percent(Function1(x), Function2(y),c)	If (Function1(x)/Function2(y)) * 100 is equal to c then elicit action to make RHS true
9	Sum(Function1(x), Function2(y),c)	If Function1(x) + Function2(y) is equal to c then elicit action to make RHS true

Example I Consider the policy "Provide provident fund to all nurses and house-keepers". This is expressed as

$$\forall x[\text{nurse}(x)\text{OR housekeeper}(x) \rightarrow \text{provide}(x, \text{PF})]$$

Range variables are

$$<\text{housekeeper}> \quad <hk>$$
$$<\text{Provident Fund}> \quad <pf>$$

Applying Guideline I

When either new nurses or new housekeepers are recruited, then a corresponding correcting action is to be taken so that RHS becomes true. Let this action be to allot provident fund. The policy enforcement rules obtained are

- WHEN recruit *n* IF !provide (*n, pf*) THEN Allot *pf*
- WHEN recruit *hk* IF !provide (*hk, pf*)THEN Allot *pf*

Applying Guideline II

Suppose provident fund is stopped for some employee. This makes RHS false. It is now required to make LHS false. This may be done by the following correcting actions:

(a) Fire nurse,
(b) Transfer nurse,
(c) Fire housekeeper, and
(d) Transfer housekeeper.

Policy enforcement rules are

- WHEN stop *pf* IF nurse(*n*) THEN Fire *n*
- WHEN stop *pf* IF nurse(*n*) THEN Transfer *n*
- WHEN stop *pf* IF housekeeper(*hk*) THEN Fire *hk*
- WHEN stop *pf* IF housekeeper(*hk*) THEN Transfer *hk*

CC-Type Policy

CC policy is a combination of CS and SC type of policies. Thus, elicitation strategies shown in Tables 4.2 and 4.4 can be applied.

Consider the following example.

Example: The total number of Wooden or Fibre Panchakarma tables must be expressed as

$$\forall x \exists wtabSet \exists ftabSet[fibreTable(x) OR\ woodTable(x)$$
$$\rightarrow Sum(count(ftabSet), count(wtabSet), 2)]$$

Here,
wtabSet: is the set of wooden tables, ftabSet: is a set of fibre tables.
Range variables are

$$<Wooden\ Table> \ <wt>$$
$$<Fibre\ Table> \ <ft>$$

Applying Guideline I

When a new wooden or fibre table is purchased, then this may disturb the total number of wooden and fibre tables in the hospital. Both LHS and RHS are complex. Applying row 9 of Table 4.2, we get

1. Elicit action to reduce the sum of tables

   (a) Discard fibre table and
   (b) Discard wooden table.

2. Elicit action to increase the sum of tables

   (a) Purchase wooden table and
   (b) Purchase fibre table.

Policy enforcement rules thus obtained are

- WHEN purchase *wt* IF !Sum(count(wtabSet),count(ftabSet),2) Then Discard *wt*
- WHEN purchase *ft* IF !Sum(count(wtabSet),count(ftabSet),2) Then Discard *ft*
- WHEN purchase *wt* IF !Sum(count(wtabSet),count(ftabSet),2) Then Purchase *wt*
- WHEN purchase *ft* IF !Sum(count(wtabSet),count(ftabSet),2) Then Purchase *ft*

Applying Guideline II

For an elicited triggering action that causes the sum to be unequal to 2, a correcting action must be elicited to make the LHS false. Let these be

(a) Discard wooden table,
(b) Stop purchasing wooden table,
(c) Discard fibre table, and
(d) Stop purchasing fibre table.

The enforcement rules are

- WHEN add *wt* IF woodTable(*wt*) THEN Discard *wt*
- WHEN add *wt* IF woodTable(*wt*) THEN Stop Purchasing *wt*
- WHEN add *wt* IF fibreTable(*ft*) THEN Discard *ft*
- WHEN add *wt* IF fibreTable(*ft*) THEN Stop Purchasing *ft*

4.3   Defining Operational Decisions

When a policy enforcement rule has been formulated, then the set of correcting actions to be taken in the organization is known. This starts off the process of arriving at operational decisions shown in Fig. 4.5. From the set of rules, correcting actions are extracted and this forms the initial choice set of actions or the initial set of decisions. Since a decision may involve other decisions, a decision is structured as a hierarchy.

From the requirements point of view, our task is to discover the operational decisions. The process shown in Fig. 4.5 is to be interpreted in this light. The set of correcting actions are high-level decisions that can be decomposed into simpler ones. The requirements engineering task is to elicit this structure.

4.3.1   Structure of an Action

The correcting action suggested by the policy enforcement rule may have its own structure. This structure is an adaptation of the AND/OR tree used in Artificial Intelligence for the reduction of problems into conjunctions and disjunctions.

Fig. 4.5 Steps in arriving at
operational decisions

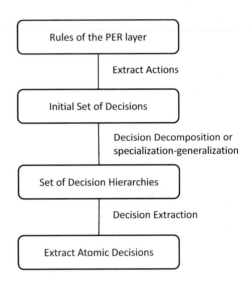

The adapted form of the AND/OR tree is as follows.

1. A node of the tree is an action. The root node is labeled with the action A_o whose structure is elaborated in the tree.
2. For every node labeled with an action A that can be decomposed into A_1 AND A_2 AND … A_n, there exists a set of children nodes N_1 AND N_2 AND … N_n such that each N_i is labeled by A_i. The nodes are conjoined by a line so as to distinguish them from other nodes that might represent other component actions of A. The line may be labeled with AND. The other nodes not conjoined are labeled with OR.

Let us illustrate the foregoing with the example shown in Fig. 4.6. The root of the tree is labeled with the action A whose structure is elaborated in the tree. A can be decomposed into conjoined actions B, C, and this yields the two nodes labeled B and C, respectively, and the line between these nodes represents the conjunction. The tree says that B AND C together form a decomposition of A.

The tree shown in Fig. 4.6 is interpreted to mean

- To do action A means that B and C must both be done,
- A is done if D is done,
- B is done if E is done, and
- B is done if F is done.

Expressed in AND/OR terms, this means that A is done by doing B AND C or (OR) by doing D. B can be done by doing E OR F.

In keeping with tradition in requirements engineering, we will use UML to represent our graphics. To represent conjoined actions, we will use the aggregation of UML labeled with AND. We will show disjoined actions by aggregation labeled with OR. Further, we will refer to all actions that can be decomposed into AND/OR

Fig. 4.6 An AND/OR action
tree

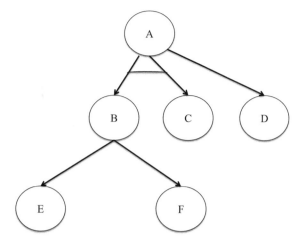

tree as complex. They will be referred to as atomic otherwise. An example of a
complex action is shown in Fig. 4.7a where *start pw* is a complex decision having
components choose department and location. These atomic actions form decisions.

We also use the notion of ISA hierarchies of UML to structure actions.
Figure 4.7b shows the ISA hierarchy rooted in the action, start private ward. The
action *start private ward* is an abstract decision with *start 2-bedded private ward*
and *start 3-bedded private ward* as its specializations.

Re-examining Fig. 4.5, each initial decision (correcting action of a PER) is sub-
jected to the AND/OR decomposition process and to the generalization–specialization process. This gives rise to decomposition and ISA hierarchies of decisions. For
each hierarchy thus obtained, the leaf nodes are determined. These leaf nodes are
atomic and thus, the set of all decisions at the operational level are obtained.

Now, the question is, for what kind of action do we need to elicit information at
the operational level? The guidelines adopted are as follows:

1. If correcting action of a rule is atomic, directly elicit information to address the
   managerial concerns outlined in Chap. 3. For example, action *expand pr* is an
   atomic action. Information relevant to it can be directly elicited.
2. If PER action is abstract, construct the IS/A hierarchy. Elicit information for
   actions in the hierarchy to address managerial concerns as above. For our action
   start private ward shown in Fig. 4.7b, information is elicited for *start private
   ward, start 2-bedded private ward,* and *start 3-bedded private ward.*
3. If PER action is complex, construct the AND/OR. Elicit information for actions
   in the hierarchy as above. Again, consider action *start private ward.* The AND/
   OR decomposition tree is constructed as shown in Fig. 4.7a and information is
   elicited for actions *start private ward, choose location,* and *choose department.*

Fig. 4.7 a Decomposition
tree for action start private
ward. **b** Specialization for
action start private ward

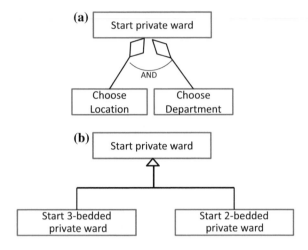

4.4 Computer-Aided Support for Obtaining Decisions

Decision elicitation and formulation is assisted by the computer-aided tool called Fetchit. Fetchit supports the interaction between the data warehouse requirements engineer and the stakeholder. It provides a comprehensive set of features for formulating policy decisions, decision for policy enforcement, the AND/OR tree of operational decisions, and also supports information elicitation. For policy decisions, domain experts identify public sources of policies and also help in determining the information required for selecting, modifying, and rejecting any policy component. Fetchit maintains a repository for holding policies and the decisions that arise from these. For PER formulation, the tool suggests the guidelines using which rules are formulated and also elicits triggering and correcting actions. The rules formulated are associated with the operators to select, modify, and reject them. For operational decisions, Fetchit guides in the construction of AND/OR trees for the correcting decisions of the rules to be enforced.

Fetchit also supports information elicitation for decisions. We shall take up this part of the tool in Chap. 5 after we have dealt with information elicitation techniques.

4.4.1 Architecture

The architecture of Fetchit can be considered in two parts as follows:

- **Front end**: This part deals with elicitation of policies, triggering, and correcting actions as well as the AND/OR tree. It also deals with the management of policies, PERs, and operational decisions. That is, all activities related to decisions and their formulation are handled in the front end of Fetchit.

- **Back end**: This part of Fetchit deals with information elicitation, maintenance of the elicited information in the information repository, and providing guidance in the information elicitation task.

The architecture of the front end of Fetchit is shown in Fig. 4.8. There are four main components, one each for the three kinds of decision-making, formulating policies, policy enforcement rules and operational decisions, and one for eliciting information. The four components are accessed via a user interface as shown in the figure. The four components interact with a repository. Let us look at the function of each component in detail.

Policy formulation: Policy formulation requires two steps, construction of the policy hierarchy and formulating the policy. The former is carried out by the policy hierarchy maker, while the latter is done by the policy formulator. These two components interact with the policy base.

The policy base is organized along two dimensions, namely policy type and domain of the organization. An organization is treated as a function with policies that govern its input, the outputs it produces, and the processing it performs to obtain the output. Consequently, there are policies to regulate input like infrastructure, material, etc.; output policies regulate the amount of output and its nature; process policies regulate the process. Besides these three policy types, there is a fourth kind that specifies the impact of the output on the organization. These are outcome policies. Now consider the domain dimension of the policy base. Here, policies can be viewed as belonging to domains such as medical, life sciences, engineering, etc.

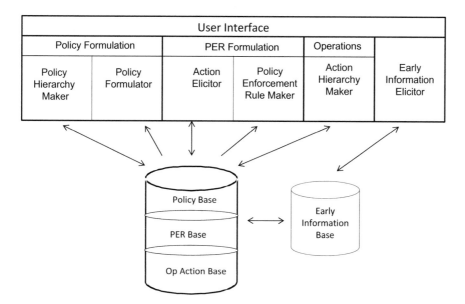

Fig. 4.8 Architecture of Fetchit

Before starting policy formulation, the requirements engineer enters the domain of the policy being formulated as well as the name of the business. The requirements engineer is given the option to view existing policies either domain-wise or policy type-wise. The third option is to retrieve based on specific terms in the policy like policies that contain the term "area".

If the domain is a new one, then the policy base returns empty handed when the domain is entered by the requirements engineer. In this case, or in the case when the engineer does not want to use legacy policies, each policy is input as an expression of the first-order logic form considered above. The logic expression is broken up into its components and the policy hierarchy is constructed by the policy hierarchy maker.

In either case, whether of reuse of policies from the database or of fresh policy input, at this stage we have policy components of interest. Now, the policy formulator presents each node of the policy hierarchy the choice to select, reject, or modify it. The formulated policies are kept in the policy base.

PER formulation: There are two parts, one the action elicitor and the another the policy enforcement rule maker. Organizational policies retrieved from the policy base are presented to the action elicitor. The action elicitor applies the two macro-guidelines and correcting and triggering actions are elicited. The PER action base is populated with elicited actions. The elicited actions are now used as input to the policy enforcement rule maker where actions are filled into the WHEN-IF-THEN form. These are then stored in the PER base. Notice that the requirements engineer role requires familiarity with extended first-order logic. This expertise may exist in the requirements engineer directly or it may be obtained through appropriately qualified experts.

Operational decisions: The PER actions in the PER action base are presented to the action hierarchy maker. New actions are discovered from the actions presented and stored in the OP action base.

Early information elicitor: The fourth component of the tool is the early information elicitor. The aim of this part is to elicit information for each decision that has been built. As already discussed, this part shall be dealt with in Chap. 5 after the information elicitation techniques have been described.

4.4.2   User Interface

Let us now consider the user interface offered by the three front end components of Fetchit, namely policy formulation, PER formulations, and operations.

Policy Formulation

There are two interfaces one each for the policy hierarchy maker and the policy formulator, respectively. These are shown in Figs. 4.9 and 4.10, respectively.

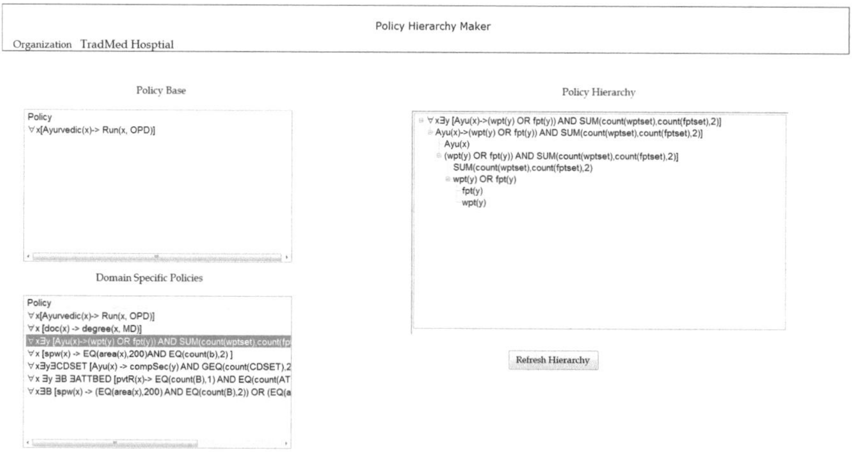

Fig. 4.9 Interface of policy hierarchy maker

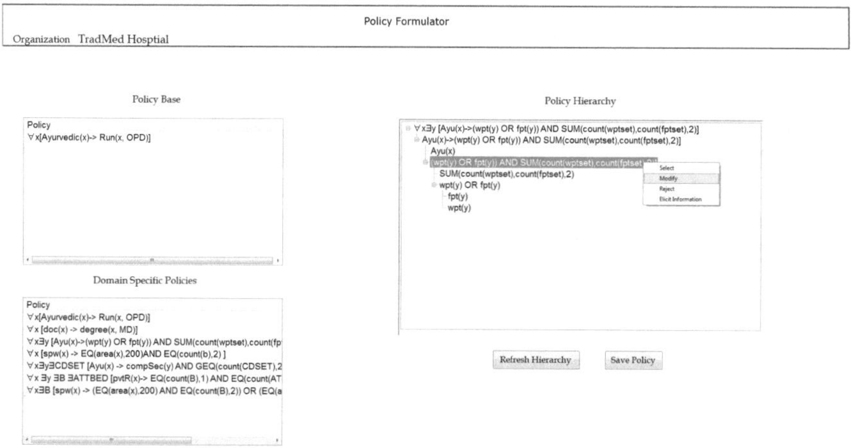

Fig. 4.10 Interface of policy formulator

As already seen, the policy hierarchy maker represents policies as hierarchies. The user interface of the policy hierarchy maker is a simple one that displays the policy and its corresponding tree. This is shown in Fig. 4.9.

The policy formulator associates select, modify, and reject with each node implicitly. Thus, it generates the set of policy decisions. The interface, see Fig. 4.10, allows the requirements engineer to select a node of the policy hierarchy and to delete it or modify it. Deletion of a node causes the sub-tree, if any, rooted in the node to be deleted. Node modification means that the label of the node is changed.

Once the policy has been formulated, the requirements engineer changes the first-order expression of the policy to reflect the policy hierarchy formulated. This statement is then stored in the policy base for later use.

PER Formulation

PER formulation consists of two components, action elicitor and the policy enforcement rule maker. We consider the user interfaces offered by Fetchit for these in turn.

The user interface of action elicitor is shown in Fig. 4.11. The policy of interest is at the top of the screen. There is provision to display existing range variables. A new range variable can be defined, by using the "Enter new Range Variable" button.

The middle panel in Fig. 4.11 is where guideline 1 is applied and right-hand side panel is where guideline 2 is applied. Existing triggering and correcting actions can be viewed by selecting "Existing actions" button. A new action can be entered by using "Insert new Action" radio button which opens a corresponding textbox.

Figure 4.11 shows the process of eliciting actions for policy, "∀x[Ayurvedic (x) → Run(x, OPD)]". In the center panel, the triggering action create x is displayed after obtaining it from the action base. Similarly, construct y is obtained and displayed. The panel also shows that the requirements engineer is entering a new correcting action start y by selecting the "Insert new Action". Guideline 2 has not yet been applied.

Let us now consider the second component of PER formulation, the policy enforcement rule maker, PER maker. This component formulates policy enforcement rules once actions have been elicited and store them in the PER base. The input to the PER maker are actions of the action base. The user interface for PER maker is shown in Fig. 4.12.

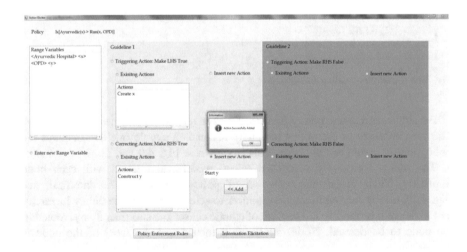

Fig. 4.11 Eliciting actions for policy "∀x[Ayurvedic(x) → Run(x, OPD)]"

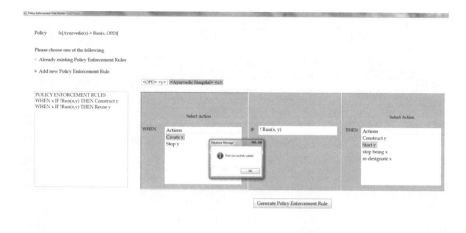

Fig. 4.12 Formulating PERs for "$\forall x[\text{Ayurvedic}(x) \rightarrow \text{Run}(x, \text{OPD})]$"

The policy for which the enforcement rules are being formulated is displayed on the top left corner of the screen in Fig. 4.12. The requirements engineer can either view already existing rules or insert a new rule. When the former is selected, a list of the rules along with the range variables present in the PER base is displayed. When the latter is selected, a panel partitioned into WHEN, IF, and THEN subsections is displayed. This partitioning corresponds to the WHEN-IF-THEN representation of the policy enforcement rules. Figure 4.12 shows the elicited triggering actions on the WHEN side, elicited correcting actions on the THEN side of the panel. The requirements engineer selects the desired triggering action from the WHEN side and the desired correcting action from the THEN side. The selected actions are highlighted. The requirements engineer keys in the IF condition. In order to save this policy enforcement rule, the Generate Policy Enforcement Rule button found at the bottom of the screen is clicked. The rule is saved in the PER base.

Operations

The Operations component consists of the action hierarchy maker. Its user interface is shown in Fig. 4.13. The screenshot of the figure is divided into three sections. The left-hand side of the screen shows the range variables and the PER actions that are from the PER action base. The upper panel on the right-hand side of the screen is where new range variable s and new actions are defined. The bottom panel of the screen is where the action hierarchy is constructed.

New actions may mean defining new range variables. For this, "Enter new Range Variable" button has been provided. On checking the radio button, new range variables can be entered. If an existing range variable can be used, "Use existing Range Variable" button is clicked. From the list provided, the necessary range variable can be selected. New actions are defined and are ready for use.

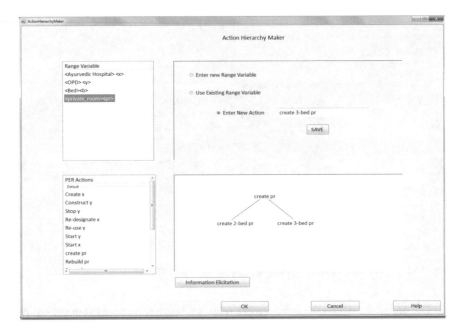

Fig. 4.13 Interface of the action hierarchy maker

4.5   Conclusion

There are three kinds of decisions, for policy formulation, PER formulation and for actions. Policy formulation decisions are obtained from policy hierarchies that display the hierarchical structure of polices. Each node of this hierarchy is associated with operators to select, reject, and modify it. Therefore, we get decisions that are three times the number of nodes in the policy hierarchy. These decisions are put through the information Elicitor part of Fetchit.

Policy enforcement rule formulation elicits triggering and correction actions from which rules are formulated. Associated with each rule are the three operators of select, reject, and modify. Thus, yet again we get a collection of decisions that are three times the number rules. Information elicitation for these is to be carried out.

Operational decisions are obtained by constructing AND/OR trees for the correcting actions of policy enforcement rules of an organization. During decision-making, choice exists in selecting between the ORed branches of the tree. Again, information is to be elicited for the actions of the AND/OR tree.

We have also seen that information elicitation is to be done for each node of the policy tree as well as for each node in the AND/OR tree. This elicitation must address the managerial concerns identified in Chap. 3. A special approach is needed for information elicitation for supporting decisions for policy enforcement rule formulation. This is because the supporting information can be directly derived from the statement of the policy for which the rule is formulated.

References

1. Lindbloom, C. E., & Woodhouse, E. J. (1993). *The policy-making process* (3rd ed.). Prentice Hall.
2. Hillman, A. J., & Hitt, M. A. (1999). Corporate political strategy formulation: A model of approach, participation, and strategy decisions. *Academy of Management Review, 24*(4), 825–842.
3. Park, Y. T. (2000). National systems of advanced manufacturing technology (AMT): Hierarchical classification scheme and policy formulation process. *Technovation, 20*(3), 151–159.
4. Kelly-Newton, L. (1980). *Accounting policy formulation: The role of corporate management*. Addison Wesley Publishing Company.
5. Ritchie, J. R. B. (1988). Consensus policy formulation in tourism: Measuring resident views via survey research. *Tourism Management, 9*(3), 199–212.
6. Cooke, P., & Morgan, K. (1993). The network paradigm: New departures in corporate and regional development. *Environment and planning D: Society and space, 11*(5), 543–564.
7. Ken, B. (2007). *Social policy: An introduction* (3rd ed.). Open University Press, Tata McGraw-Hill.
8. Wies, R. (1994). Policy definition and classification: Aspects, criteria, and examples. In *International Workshop on Distributed Systems: Operations & Management*, Toulouse, France, October 10–12, pp. 1–12.
9. Anderson, C. (2005). What's the difference between policies and procedures? *Bizmanualz*.
10. OMG. (2008). *Semantics of business vocabulary and business rules (SBVR)*, v1.0, January 2008.
11. The Business Rules Group. (2010). *The business motivation model: Business governance in a volatile world*, Release 1.4.
12. Leite, J. C. S. P., & Leonardi, M. C. (1998, April). Business rules as organizational policies. In *Software Specification and Design* (pp. 68–76). IEEE.
13. Fu, G., Shao, J., Embury, S. M., Gray, W. A., & Liu, X. (2001). A framework for business rule presentation. In *Proceedings of 12th International Workshop on Database and Expert Systems Applications*, 2001 (pp. 922–926). IEEE.
14. Auechaikul, T., & Vatanawood, W. (2007). A development of business rules with decision tables for business processes. In *TENCON 2007–2007 IEEE Region 10 Conference* (pp 1–4). IEEE.
15. Muehlen, M. Z., & Kamp, G. (2007). Business process and business rule modeling: A representational analysis. In *Eleventh International IEEE on EDOC Conference Workshop, 2007, EDOC07* (pp. 189–196). IEEE.
16. Rosca, D., Greenspan, S., Feblowitz, M., & Wild, C. (1997). A decision making methodology in support of the business rules lifecycle. In *Proceedings of the Third IEEE International Symposium on Requirements Engineering*, 1997 (pp. 236–246). IEEE.
17. Navathe, S. B., Elmasri, R., & James, L. (1986). Integrating user views in database design. *IEEE Computer, 19*, 50–62.

Chapter 5
Information Elicitation

Having looked at the processes using which decisions can be determined, we now move on to the second aspect of DWRE mentioned in Chap. 3, namely, that of eliciting information relevant to each decision. Decisions represent the useful work that is supported by the data warehouse. This work can be to formulate policies, policy enforcement rules, or to take operational decisions. The decision–information association is important because it defines the purpose served by the data warehouse. We use this association for defining the notion of a decision requirement that forms the basis of our information elicitation technique.

We have seen in Chap. 3 that DWRE would benefit from systematization of the information elicitation process. To explicitly identify the benefit, we now examine in greater detail the methods used by different DWRE techniques. Since stakeholder–requirements engineer interaction is paramount, we lay down four basic principles that, if followed, led to good quality interaction. Thereafter, we formulate the life cycle of decisional data warehouse development and then go on to describe our information elicitation approach.

5.1 Obtaining Multidimensional Structure

DWRE methods presented in Chap. 2 treat the definition of facts and dimensions of the data warehouse to be built as part of the requirements engineering process. These methods adopt a variable number of steps in the process of reaching the multidimensional, MD structure of the data warehouse.

Table 5.1 shows that there can be between one-step and three-step processes in DWRE methods. **One-step processes** are based on the idea that enough information should be obtained as early as possible to arrive at the MD structure. This is the view of methods in the fourth, fifth, sixth, and ninth rows of the table. That is, as soon as a stakeholder determines that a piece of information is relevant in the data warehouse, these methods immediately identify whether it is a fact or a dimension.

© Springer Nature Singapore Pte Ltd. 2018
N. Prakash and D. Prakash, *Data Warehouse Requirements Engineering*,
https://doi.org/10.1007/978-981-10-7019-8_5

Table 5.1 Arriving at the MD structure

S. No.	DWRE method	Elicitation process		
		Step 1	Step 2	Step 3
1	Boehlein M., Ulbrich-vom E. A.	Build SERM	Build MD structure	
2	Bonifati A., Ceri S., Fuggetta A., Paraboschi S.	Elicit quality focus, variation factors, and baseline hypothesis	Build MD structure	
3	Paim F.R.S., Castro J.B., Prakash N., Singh Y., and Gosain	Information scenarios	Build ER diagram	Build MD structures
4	Georgini P., Rizzi S., and Garzetti M.	Build MD structure		
5	Gam I. and Salinesi C.	Build MD structure		
6	Mazon J.N., Pardillo J., and Trujillo J.	Build MD structure		
7	Prakash N. and Bhardwaj H	Use case diagrams	Build ER diagram	Build MD structures
8	Corr L. and Stagnitto J.	Tables	Build MD structures	
9	Hughes R.	Build MD structure		

There is overriding concern on the data model of the data warehouse to-be. The process of obtaining information and conversion of elicited information into facts/dimensions is completely implicit, unarticulated and unsystematic.

In contrast, multistep processes break up the complex requirements engineering task into relatively more manageable pieces. Each step focuses on a single aspect of the task, obtaining information, building a conceptual schema, and constructing the MD structure respectively. Consequently, it is possible to develop techniques to address the concerns of each step. Let us now take up such multistep processes.

Two-step approaches are shown in the first, second, and third rows of Table 5.1. The piece of information acquired from the stakeholder is initially represented in some generic form in the first step, and is then converted into the MD structure. In the method of row 1, the method is to obtain service measures from stakeholders that they map to SERM in step one and then get the MD structure from the SERM diagram. In the method of the third row, information obtained from abstraction sheets as quality focus, variation factors, etc. in step one is converted to the MD structure in step 2. The method of row 8 suggests obtaining information in the form of tables before building the MD structure.

The two-step process separates the issues of obtaining information and its initial representation from building the MD structure. The manner of conversion from the former to the latter can be studied and systematized. Thus, for example, algorithms like the one developed by [1–3] for converting from ER schema to MD guide in this conversion task.

Three-step processes, see rows three and seven of Table 5.1, provide a process step for the stakeholder to articulate the needed information. In the method of the third row, a typical interaction between the decision-maker and the information elicitation system is represented as an information scenario. During this interaction, the decision-maker formulates typical queries to obtain information in an SQL-like language. This information is then represented as an ER schema for later conversion into MD structures. The method in the seventh row of the table obtains the key performance indicators, KPIs, of a decision-maker, treats these as functions, and then determines the input parameters of these functions and the output produced. Inputs and outputs are the needed information. This method develops a variant of use cases of UML. Again, an ER schema is built that is converted to MD structure.

Three-step processes move away from merely structuring information to obtaining information from the stakeholder and then structuring it. They attempt to systematize the entire task right from information elicitation through defining MD structures.

However, these processes do not provide guidance and support in the task of information elicitation. Thus, for example, in the informational scenario approach, the manner in which the SQL-like query is identified and the response formulated is not articulated.

5.2   Decisional Information Elicitation

Our decisional information elicitation technique is developed to provide guidance and support in the information elicitation task. In doing so, it factors-in the issues and concerns raised in Chap. 3.

We define decisional information elicitation as the process of obtaining from decision-makers the information relevant to the each identified decision. It is a generic process and can be applied to any kind of decision identified in Chap. 4. Thus, we can obtain information about policy formulation, policy enforcement rule formulation as well as operational decisions.

Decisional information elicitation is carried out through stakeholder–requirements engineer interaction. A good quality interaction is that which is

1. Effective in the sense that it identifies all the relevant information without missing out any relevant information.
2. Efficient in the sense that there is no meandering, unfocused interaction that unnecessarily uses up stakeholder and requirements engineer time.
3. Guided so as to ensure that the interaction is proceeding along the right lines, raising and obtaining responses to important issues.

To achieve good quality interaction, the decisional information elicitation process follows four principles as follows:

(a) Stakeholder buy-in. It should be apparent to stakeholders that the elicitation process addresses their managerial concerns and the data warehouse under development shall be beneficial. This assures continued and sustained interest of the stakeholder in the elicitation task. Such interest is necessary because information elicitation is a long, time-consuming process and requires sustained concentration.

(b) 360° view of information. Stakeholders should be encouraged to think of their information needs in the broad perspective of their all-round activities. Often, perhaps, due to personal viewpoints or operational pressures, managers offer only a limited perspective of their information needs. The elicitation process must be such as to provide a range of viewpoints, explicitly offering the stakeholder the option of providing information from each viewpoint.

(c) Early information. Stakeholders are not particularly concerned about the structure of the information. On the other hand, technical people, requirements engineers, system designers, and implementers have large stakes in developing the right data models and structures. The information elicitation technique should not impose a technical concern on stakeholders. In other words, the information elicitation process should determine "early" information. This early information is unstructured perhaps just a name so as to provide a placeholder to accommodate it. It is devoid of any metadata like data type, data length, and other such details. Similarly, whether this information is already available in OLTP systems or not and whether it is to be obtained from external sources are not interesting issues here. These shall be addressed when the data model design for the data warehouse shall be taken up.

(d) Model-driven: Eliciting early information could become a "fishing and roving" exercise in the absence of a model. Therefore, elicitation process must be model-driven. This implies that the stakeholder–requirements engineer interaction is carried out with the specific intention of populating the concepts of the early information model. Therefore, questionnaires, interviews, and brainstorming sessions are designed to elicit responses containing instances of model concepts. This provides guidance to requirements engineers in the information elicitation task, namely, to ask for only model-specific information.

The foregoing principles ensure that stakeholder–requirements engineer interaction is of good quality as defined earlier. We see that the information elicitation process based on the foregoing principles has properties as follows:

1. It guides stakeholder–requirements engineer interaction. For the requirements engineer, this means that the various viewpoints comprising the 360° view must all be explored with stakeholders. Since the elicitation process is for early information, the elicitation process keeps the requirements engineer–stakeholder interaction away from issues around information structures, metadata, whether

or not information is already available, and consideration of information sources. Thus, the interaction moves along desired lines.

2. It is effective and efficient. The stakeholder is constrained to provide information that goes into model instantiation only. Thus, extraneous concerns and discussions are minimized. Further, the elicitation process is comprehensive. This makes stakeholders adopt the 360° view of information thereby increasing the possibility of obtaining "all" information and reducing the possibility of missing information.

The place of our information elicitation technique in the decisional data warehouse development life cycle is shown in Table 5.2. The requirements engineering stage in this life cycle consists of three substages. The decision formulation substage was explained in Chap. 4 and its purpose is to obtain policy formulation, PER formulation, and operational decisions. We saw that the input to this stage can be reusable policies for producing policy formulation decisions, policies for PER formulation decisions, and actions of policy enforcement rules for producing operational decisions respectively.

The early information substage is entirely concerned with eliciting information from stakeholders. At the end of this substage, early information relevant to decisions gets identified in accordance with an early information model. This information is then used in the third substage, the late information substage to construct an ER schema.

The conceptual design stage of the life cycle aims to develop the multidimensional model. It takes the ER schema produced by the late information substage and produces the multidimensional model in an implementation-independent manner. This multidimensional model is finally converted, in the logical design stage, into the MOLAP/ROLAP schema of the particular data warehouse development platform being used.

Table 5.2 The decisional data warehouse development life cycle

Stage	Substage	Input	Output
Requirements engineering	Decision formulation	Policies, PERs, goals	Decisions
	Early information	Decisions	Early information
	Late information	Early information	ER schema
Conceptual design		ER schema	Multidimensional model
Logical design		Multidimensional model	MOLAP/ROLAP structure

5.3   The Decision Requirement Model

Our information elicitation technique uses the decision requirement model [4]. This model captures in it the structure of a decision and of information respectively as well as the relationship between these two. Information that is relevant to a decision is represented in the decision requirement model as a decision requirement. This association is textually written as <decision, information>. In Fig. 5.1, it is modeled as an aggregation of decision and information respectively. The decision–information relationship is N:M since a decision may have more than one information associated with it and a given information may be associated with more than one decision.

5.3.1   The Notion of a Decision

As already seen in earlier chapters, a decision is a member of a choice set. In Fig. 5.1, we represent this by the relationship, *is member of*, between choice set and decision. A decision can participate in more than one choice set and a choice set can have several decisions as its members. This implies that *is member of* is an N:M relationship. A choice set is associated with a situation. This is modeled by defining the relationship, *relevant to*, in Fig. 5.1. A situation models the current state of the organization and is a trace of what has been happening in the organization in the past.

Consider a health service that has a large rush of patients. The situation, the trace of the organization, may show that a number of patients were admitted and a number of them were turned away. To handle this situation, the decision-maker associates a choice set with this situation. The choice set is

Fig. 5.1 The decision requirements metamodel

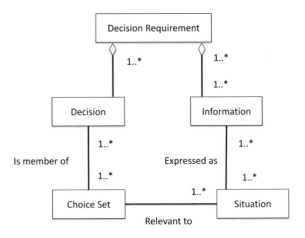

Reduce patient rush = {register patients online, increase medical staff}.

The first member of this choice set aims to reduce the physical rush of patients on site, whereas the second member of the choice set is for handling of a larger number of patients on site.

Figure 5.1 shows an N:M relationship between choice set and decision. The choice set considered above consists of more than one decision. Further, the first member of Reduce patient rush, namely, register patients online, can be a member in another choice set say, for improving the medical services. This shows the N:M relationship.

The figure also shows a 1:N relationship between choice set and situation. That is, a choice set is applicable to many situations but a situation has only one choice set associated with it. In our example, there is one choice set associated with the situation to handle the rush of patients. However, this choice set can also be applicable to the situation that requires improvement of medical services.

There are two constraints, namely, coherence and cardinality constraints on a choice set. **Coherence** ensures that all elements of a choice set must achieve the same purpose. Consider the choice set, CSET = {Increase bed count, Optimize bed use, Increase units}. All members of this set have the same purpose, namely, to reduce the rush of patients. This choice set is coherent. An example of an incoherent choice set is CSET1 = {Increase bed count, Optimize bed use, Open research unit}. The member, open research unit, does not help in reducing the rush of patients. Therefore, CSET1 is incoherent.

The **cardinality** says that the number of members of a choice set must be greater than unity. Clearly, a choice set with no alternatives, that is, having cardinality = 0 is undefined. If this cardinality = 1, then there is exactly one alternative and there is no decisional problem. For a decision problem to exist, it is necessary that the cardinality of the choice set should be greater than unity. The cardinality constraint ensures that this is indeed so.

Figure 5.1 shows the relationship between situation and information. This is an M:N relationship.

5.3.2 Metamodel of Decisions

The decision metamodel, expressed in UML notation, shows three kinds of decisions: Atomic, abstract, and complex. An atomic decision cannot be decomposed into subdecisions. An abstract decision is arrived at by using generalization/specialization principles to produce ISA relationships between decisions. Finally, a complex decision is composed of other simpler decisions. Complex decisions form an AND/OR hierarchy. This is captured in Fig. 5.2 by the concept, Link that can be an AND or an OR. These subtypes of links are not shown in the figure.

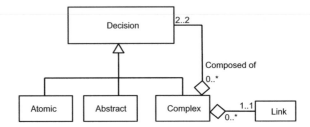

Fig. 5.2 The metamodel of decisions

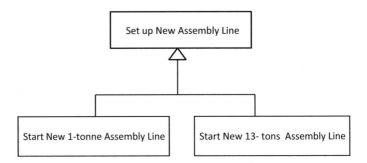

Fig. 5.3 An abstract decision

Let us illustrate an abstract decision. Consider an automobile plant that makes 1-tonne and 13-tonne trucks. The organization, faced with increased demand, considers the possibility of building a new assembly line of trucks. This gives rise to the decision, *Set up New Assembly Line* that is specialized into two decisions, *Start New 1-tonne Line* and *Start New 13-tonne Line,* respectively. This is modeled as ISA relationships with *Set up New Assembly Line* as shown in Fig. 5.3.

The introduction of an abstract decision is motivated by the consideration as follows. It is possible to treat the specialized classes of an ISA hierarchy as flat structures by introducing attributes in atomic/complex classes, and, vice versa, it is possible to convert classes with common attributes into an ISA hierarchy. Thus, whether hierarchical abstraction is used or not in a particular situation is only determined by the clarity that it brings to a schema. An ISA hierarchy brings out commonality explicitly, which remains hidden if an attribute is used instead of it.

Our inclusion of an abstract decision provides for explicit representation of ISA structures as exemplified by the generalization, *Set up New Assembly Line* of *Start New 1-tonne Line* and *Start New 13-tonne Line,* respectively. These latter two decisions inherit the properties *Set up New Assembly Line.*

Now, the decision *Set up New Assembly Line* is also a complex decision having two components, *Create separate profit centre* and *Merge with existing profit centre* (see Fig. 5.4a). An OR link connects these two components.

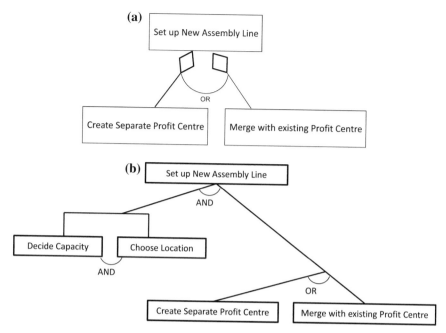

Fig. 5.4 a A complex decision with OR link, **b** a complex decision

Figure 5.4b shows an example of a complex decision with a combination of AND/OR links. Two more components are shown, *Decide Capacity* and *Choose Location,* with an AND link. That is, the decision to *Set up New Assembly Line* requires that both the capacity and the location of the assembly line should be decided. The OR link between *Create separate profit centre* and *Merge with existing profit centre* says that only one of these two is to be selected. Finally, the structure shown in Fig. 5.4b says that setting up of the new line involves three decisions, the two decisions to decide capacity and location as well as the third decision to either create a separate profit center or to merge with an existing one.

5.3.3 Information

The notion of information is also explained in Fig. 5.1. The detailed information model [4] is shown in Fig. 5.5. Let there be a set of decisions $D = \{D1, D2... Dn\}$. Each Di, $1 \leq i \leq n$, is a member of its own choice set and is associated with its relevant information. Consequently, we can associate, with each Di, its relevant information represented by Ii. Then, the set of relevant information to D, represented as information in Fig. 5.5, is defined as the union of these information sets:

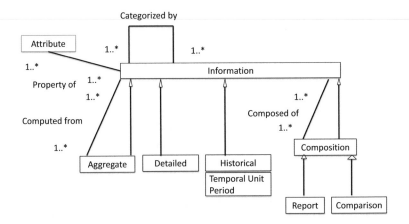

Fig. 5.5 The information metamodel

$$\text{Information} = \text{I1} \cup \text{I2} \ldots \cup \text{In}$$
$$= \{\text{I such that I belongs to Ip, } 1 \leq p \leq n\}$$

Now, data warehouse technology tells us that there are three kinds of information, detailed information, summarized or aggregated information, and historical information. All these different kinds of information have their own dimensions.

Figure 5.5 expresses this through a typology of information. This typology is shown in Fig. 5.5 by the ISA links between *Information* and *Detailed*, *Aggregate*, and *Historical* information. Detailed information is raw unprocessed information. Aggregate information is obtained by computing from other detailed, aggregate, or historical information. This is modeled by the "Computed from" relationship between aggregate and information. *Historical* information is defined by its two properties, period or duration of the history (5, 10, etc.) and temporal unit that tells us the time unit, month, quarter etc., for which history is to be maintained.

Figure 5.5 shows a special kind of information called composition. The idea of composition is to define a meaningful collection of logically related information. There are two kinds of compositions, namely, reports and comparisons as represented by the ISA links between these. A report is built from logically related detailed, aggregate or historical information as well as of comparisons. A comparison is a composition of information that enables the decision-maker to compare organizational data. It may contain rankings like top ten, bottom 10, or may bring out the similarities/differences between a variety of information.

The specific properties of information are modeled as attributes. There is an N:M relationship between attribute and information as shown in Fig. 5.5.

Finally, Fig. 5.5 shows the notion of dimension by defining a relationship, *Categorized by*. This recursive relationship is N:M and allows categories of information to be formed with respect to other information. Thus, we get sales by season, where sales and season are two instances of information.

5.4   Eliciting Information

The problem of eliciting decision requirements is that of obtaining all information relevant to a decision. Therefore, in an enterprise-wide data warehouse, information relevant to all the decisions in the set D must be available.

We associate an elicitation technique with each factor that promotes manger buy-in as discussed in Chap. 3. Consequently, there are four such techniques, namely, CSFI, ENDSI, MEANSI, and outcome feedback [4, 5]. The first step in eliciting information is to obtain the relevant achievement parameter for a decision. Thereafter, it is necessary to determine the variables used to measure/estimate the achievement. As the third a final step, the required information for estimating the achievement must be elicited.

5.4.1   CSFI Elicitation

The CSFI elicitation technique elicits information required to estimate achievement in critical work areas. It requires elicitation of the variables that should be monitored to assess this achievement.

Table 5.3 shows the nature of the CSFI technique. The first three columns contain the decision, CSF, and the variables for measuring the CSF. Finally, the fourth column contains the elicited information relevant to the CSF variables.

The example presented in Table 5.3 is for the decision of adding a new pharmacy in the health service. The CSF associated with it are medicine delivery time and medicine availability. One variable of each is shown in the table. For the

Table 5.3 Eliciting information from CSFI

Decision	CSF	CSF variable	Information
Add new pharmacy	Medicine delivery time	Waiting time of patient	**Aggregate**: average waiting time **Category**: patient type **History**: *time unit*: month *Duration* quarter
	Medicine availability	Non-availability	**Aggregate**: number of times of non-availability

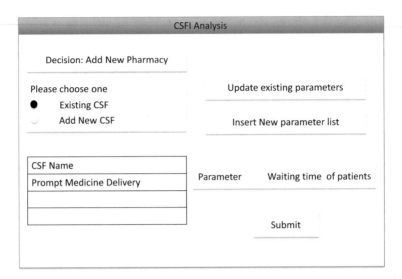

Fig. 5.6 The CSFI interface

former, the needed information is the average waiting time categorized by patient type. A monthly record of this information is to be kept for a quarter.

The table implies that CSFI elicitation is done in three steps, (a) CSF association with a decision is elicited, (b) CSF variables are obtained, and (c) information is identified to populate the model shown in Fig. 5.5. The interface of the elicitation tool for CSFI elicitation is shown in Fig. 5.6.

The figure shows that elicitation is being done for the decision add new pharmacy. The interface allows (a) selection of a CSF from the list of CSFs displayed or (b) to enter a new CSF. The figure shows that the CSF, Prompt medicine delivery, has been selected and the variable, waiting time for patients, has been entered. A subsequent screen, not shown here, then obtains the information detailed in the fourth column of Table 5.3.

5.4.2   ENDSI Elicitation

ENDSI elicitation is for obtaining information so as to estimate the effectiveness of an end. Table 5.4 shows that similar to CSFI, there are four aspects of ENDSI elicitation. In the first three columns, we have the decision, the End, and the effectiveness variables. Finally, the last column contains the relevant information.

Table 5.4 ENDSI elicitation

Decision	End	End effectiveness variable	Information
Add new pharmacy	Full utilization	Customer service provided	**Aggregate**: amount of sales **category**: medicine-wise
			Aggregate: count of transactions **Category**: shift-wise

Again, consider the same decision of adding a new pharmacy but for estimating achievement of the Ends. The End associated with it is full utilization. An effectiveness variable for assessing the effectiveness of full utilization is the customer service provided. The information needed for this variable is the total amount of sales for each medicine sold by the pharmacy. The table shows that the variable can also be estimated by keeping information of the number of transactions carried out during each shift.

Though not brought out in the example here, it is possible for a decision to have several Ends. Each End can have several variables.

5.4.3 MEANSI Elicitation

Means information elicitation is for eliciting information needed to evaluate the efficiency of the means. Requirements engineer/stakeholder interaction is for eliciting variables and associated information that help in estimating the efficiency of the means adopted.

Again, we see the four-column structure in Table 5.5: the first two columns associate the means with a decision, the third captures the variable for the efficiency of the means, and finally, information is obtained.

The example in Table 5.5 is again for the same decision, add new pharmacy. The means are to start completely afresh or to reuse an existing building. The

Table 5.5 Obtaining information from MEANSI elicitation

Decision	Means	Means efficiency variable	Information
Add new pharmacy	Establish afresh	Resources created	Estimated cost Category: resource-wise
		Time	Setting up time
	Reuse existing building	Resources used	Reused resources Category: resource-wise
			Operational time

Table 5.6 Output feedback information

Decision	Feedback variable	Information
Add new pharmacy	Increase in patients	**Aggregate**: count of patients **Category**: speciality-wise **History**: time unit: year Duration: 1
	Increased medical staff	**Aggregate**: count of additional doctors **Category**: speciality-wise

efficiency variables for the former are shown in the table. These are the resources that shall be created and include civil work, electrical work, fixtures and furniture, equipment, etc. The information needed is the estimation of cost for each resource that shall be provided. The second row of the table shows another variable, Time, for the required time to establish the new pharmacy.

The second means is estimated by the extent of reuse of existing resources and the time to become operational.

5.4.4   Feedback Information Elicitation

Feedback information elicitation aims to determine the impact of a decision and each element impacted is seen to be a variable. As before, the information for the variable is then elicited. As shown in Table 5.6, the three aspects of interest are the decision, the feedback variable that captures the impact, and the information to be kept.

Consider, again, the same decision add new pharmacy. Adding the new pharmacy has the effect of creating a better perception of our health service. This change has resulted in an increase in the number of registered patients that in turn leads to addition of a new pharmacy. The second variable says that in order to keep the new pharmacy fully utilized, additional medical staff may be required that in turn affects the number of pharmacies. This feedback cycle starts from the outcome of add new pharmacy and returns back to it.

Table 5.6 shows the feedback variables and the information required.

5.5   The Global Elicitation Process

The techniques described in Sect. 5.4 have their own elicitation process consisting of two or three steps. We have provided details of this micro-level guided process. However, as mentioned, the use of multiple elicitation techniques, corresponding to the factors of interest, shall be beneficial. This implies that there is a global, macro-level elicitation process that suggests interleaving of these micro-level processes.

Our global, multi-factor elicitation process takes as input the set of decisions, D and, each decision of D guides the requirements engineer to determine the relevant achievement parameter, namely, CSF, etc. The micro-level elicitation technique(s) associated with each factor are then deployed.

This determination can be done in different ways as follows:

(a) Decision-wise: This process of determining information picks up a decision from D and then applies each technique, one after the other. After all the techniques have been applied, then the next decision is taken up. The process ends when information elicitation has been carried out for all decisions in the set.

   This process has the benefit that it minimizes the number of visits to the stakeholder for obtaining the required information. This is because, in principle, all information can be obtained about the decision in one sitting. Therefore, if stakeholders can be available for long sessions, then this technique works well. An additional session, in all probability, will be required for verification purposes.

(b) Sliced decision-wise: This is a variant of the decision-wise process in which information elicitation is done from only one of the four elicitation techniques. The sliced decision-wise process needs several, relatively shorter duration requirements engineer–stakeholder sessions. At the beginning of each session, the previous work done could be verified.

(c) Technique-wise: This process gives primacy to the information elicitation technique. The requirements engineer selects one of the four techniques and applies it to the decisions of D, one by one. The process ends when all the techniques have been applied to all decisions of D.

   This process requires several sessions with each stakeholder. Each session is shorter than the one in the decision-wise process. This process works well when stakeholders cannot be available for a long interactive session but can give several shorter duration appointments. At the beginning of each session, the previous work done could be checked out for correctness.

(d) Sliced technique-wise: This process breaks up the technique-wise process into smaller parts. When a stakeholder has a stake in more than one decision in D, then there are two aspects to these processes that are interesting. These are as follows:

   • The stakeholder is guided to examine the relevance of all the factors and encouraged to do complete requirements analysis.
   • The stakeholder can prioritize the factors considered important.

Indeed, as we will see in the example later in this chapter, decisions for formulating policies rely heavily on CSFI and ENDSI, respectively. However, MEANSI is not so relevant, perhaps, because the means in this case are the policy enforcement rules since, evidently, these rules enforce policies.

5.6   Eliciting Information for Policy Decision-Making

Let us illustrate the use of the four elicitation techniques for formulating policies. Consider the policy that for all in-patient departments, IPD, there must be at least one doctor with the degree MD and the number of doctors must be at least 2. Let the range variable of doctor be y and let the condition on doctors be captured by the predicates degree (y, MD) and GEQ (count(D),2). The expression in the first-order logic, as discussed in Chap. 4, is as follows:

$$\forall x \exists y \exists D[IPD(x) \rightarrow doc(y) \text{ AND } GEQ(count(D),2) \text{ AND } degree(y, MD)].$$

The hierarchy of this policy is shown in Fig. 5.7.

5.6.1   CSFI Elicitation

For our example policy shown in Fig. 5.7, let there be a CSF, "patient satisfaction". Now, the hierarchy is traversed in the left to right, bottom-up manner. For each node thus obtained, the information needed to assess CSF achievement is elicited.

For the node IPD(x), we get patient satisfaction measures for the in-patient department as follows:

- Rate of patient admission,
- Prompt provision of medical aid,
- Availability of paramedical services,
- Rapidity of discharge procedure, and
- Referrals to other hospitals.

Fig. 5.7 Policy hierarchy

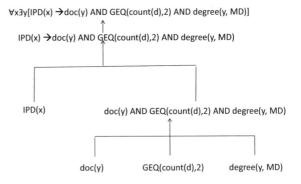

Thereafter aggregates, history requirements, etc. are obtained.

Now, we move to the next node, doc(y). Information relevant to satisfaction of "patient satisfaction" elicited is

(i)   number of doctors specialization-wise,
(ii)   experience of each doctor, or doctor-wise experience, and
(iii)   doctor availability per patient.

The information obtained through CSFI elicitation is kept in the early information base shown in Fig. 5.11. The structure of the early information base is as follows. Information of the model becomes entity, Attribute becomes attribute; Historical properties are stored in History field of the early information base, Categorized by property in the Category field, and finally, aggregate required in the Function field of the early information base.

Figure 5.8 shows the user interface of the elicitation tool for the decision node doc(y). The top shows the node, doc(y), for which information is being elicited. Below this are the two options, to select an existing CSF or to add a new CSF. The figure shows a newly added CSF, Patient Satisfaction. Further, assessment of the CSF can be done by examining the information, Doctor, together with its attribute, Degree. It is shown that

• Information is categorized by specialization of the doctor.
• The function to be applied is count.
• History is to be maintained for each month.

This process continues till the root of the policy hierarchy is reached and its information has been elicited.

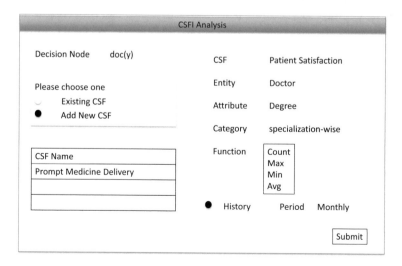

Fig. 5.8 CSFI elicitation

5.6.2   Ends Information Elicitation

For our policy shown in Fig. 5.7, let one of the ends be to provide comprehensive patient service. The next step is to get hold of the effectiveness measures of this end. This is done by traversing the hierarchy as before.

Consider IPD(x). For our ends, we get measures

- Referrals to other medical services and
- Medical services that are rented.

For each of these, we now elicit the information for evaluating it. For the former, we get

- Number of operations performed every day and their history for 1-year period;
- Number of referrals every day; history for 1 year;
- Case of each referral; and
- Inward referrals by other medical facilities.

Thereafter, the second effectiveness measure, medical services rented, is taken up.

As before, the elicited information is used to populate the information model and elicited information is stored in the early information base shown in Fig. 5.11.

5.7   Eliciting Information for PER Formulation

In order to formulate policy enforcement rules, we need to analyze the policy concerned. As discussed in Chap. 4, the expression of the policy is picked up to determine the ways in which the policy can be violated and correcting actions are obtained. Policy violation occurs when the left-hand side of the policy expression is true but the right-hand side of the expression is false. Clearly, information must be kept in the PER data warehouse fragment to know if the left-hand side of the policy expression is true or false. Similarly, we must keep information to know if the right-hand side of the expression is true/false.

Early information needed can be identified by considering the variables, functions, and predicates of the policy expression. Since these refer to their corresponding real-world phenomena, we need to obtain information about the real-world phenomena referred to.

Consider the general form of a policy

$$\text{Quantifiers (IF } F_1 \text{ THEN } F_2)$$

Both F_1 and F_2 can be complex. As defined in Chap. 4, this means that F_1 and F_2 can both have conjunctions, disjunctions, and n-adic functions.

The information elicitation task is to obtain information referred to by the formulae F_1 and F_2, respectively. Here, the role of bound variables is critical. Consider the predicate P(x) where x is bound. This suggests to us that information about the real-world phenomena denoted by P must be elicited. For example, consider the left-hand side of a policy as follows:

$$\forall x[\text{spw}(x) \rightarrow \ldots]$$

Recall that spw denotes a semi-private ward. Therefore, we can surmise that we need information of **all** semi-private wards.

Now, let us assume a different quantification as follows:

$$\exists x[\text{spw}(x) \rightarrow \ldots]$$

Here, we need to obtain information to ascertain that there is at least one spw meeting the condition on the right-hand side. Again, we need to obtain information about **all** semi-private wards in order to do so. Therefore, it can be seen that irrespective of the whether universal or existential quantification is used, information about all semi-private wards is of interest.

A reading of the policy may also suggest the specific information required. For example, consider

$$\forall x[\text{nurse}(x) \text{ AND GEQ}(\text{salary}(x), \ 15000) \rightarrow \ldots]$$

This says that information about all nurses is needed and more specifically we need their salary.

Lastly, when a formula contains a function, then either the value of the function must be computed on demand or its value must be available in the data warehouse.

A full reading of the policy helps to determine the nature of the required information. For example, consider the policy as follows:

$$\forall x \exists B[\text{spw}(x) \text{ AND bed}(B) \rightarrow \text{EQ}(\text{count}(B),2)$$
$$\text{AND EQ}(\text{area}(x),200) \text{ AND belongs}(x, B)]$$

Here, B is a complex variable; bed is a predicate that returns true if the collection in B are all beds; area is a function that computes the area of x; count is a function that counts the number of B; and belongs is a predicate that returns true if B belongs to x. The quantification suggests that we need to keep information about semi-private wards and collections of beds. However, the predicate, belongs, clarifies that the collection of beds is to be for each semi-private ward, that is spw-wise. We need to consider whether the area of a semi-private ward shall be stored or shall be calculated each time it is needed. In the latter case, enough information, for example, length and breadth, will need to be determined. A similar view is to be adopted for the function, count. Should we keep the count of beds or will we compute it dynamically when needed.

It can be seen that information elicitation for PER formulation can be done directly from an interpretation of the policy as expressed in the first-order logic of Chap. 4. The only issue is of determining whether historical information is needed or not. This cannot be ascertained from the first-order expression. Therefore, interaction with the PER decision-maker should be carried out to determine any requirements for history. There is no need to deploy the four elicitation techniques here.

5.8 Information Elicitation for Operational Systems

Lastly, let us consider information elicitation for operational decisions. Operational decision-making is a two-step process:

1. Determine which rule is to be applied. For example, consider the two policy enforcement rules as follows:

   WHEN stop y IF ayH(a) THEN stop a
   WHEN stop y IF ayH(a) THEN re-designate a

   The decision-maker needs to select one of the two rules and commit to either stop a or to re-designate a.
2. Now interest is in determining the manner in which the action of the PER, stop a, or re-designate a, shall be implemented. As discussed in Chap. 4, the AND/OR structure of the action is picked up and the DW fragment consulted. Therefore, the information elicited must be relevant to each decision in the AND/OR structure.

5.8.1 Elicitation for Selecting PER

Information elicitation for the first step is illustrated below. As shown, unlike information elicitation for PER formulation, the techniques developed in Sect. 5.4 are used here. We illustrate this for eliciting information for the second rule above, that is, for the action re-designate a, where a is an instance of AYUSH hospital.

1. **CSFI Analysis**: As discussed earlier, a CSF is to provide patient satisfaction. To assess this factor, one piece of information needed is the total yearly count of patients. This gives rise to the decision requirement <Re-designate x, annual number of patients>. Applying the information model, Patient becomes Entity.
2. **ENDSI Analysis**: The objective or result of re-designate a can be to maximize economic return. The effectiveness of this end can be assessed by Revenue generated, that is estimated by cost per lab test, number of tests, service fees of nurses, and consultancy fees of doctors. Applying the information model, lab

test, doctor, and nurse become entities with service fees and consultancy fees as attributes for nurse and doctor entity, respectively.

3. **MEANSI Analysis**: Again consider the action "Re-designate a", where a is an instance of AYUSH hospital. One means to perform this action is to re-designate the hospital by choosing another speciality. The efficiency with which this is done is determined by the expertise available already in the hospital. If enough expertise is available, then the re-designation shall be efficiently carried out. Early information needed is about number of doctors having the specialized qualification, number of patients with disease of the speciality, and current equipment in the hospital in the area of the speciality, among others. Again, applying the information model, doctor, patient, disease, and equipment become entities.

The results of performing steps 1–3 above are summarized in Table 5.7. The table has two columns, the first column for the information elicitation techniques being applied to the action, re-designate x, and the second column describes the information base.

The early information base contains variables obtained from CSFI, ENDSI, and MEANSI. For each measure, entity, attribute, history, category, and function are identified as part of the information base.

5.8.2   Information Elicitation for Actions

The second step in operational decision-making is that of selecting the micro-level decisions involved in realizing the action of the selected PER. There are two interesting cases depending on whether the nature of the action is atomic or complex.

Atomic

If the action is atomic, then it cannot be decomposed into the AND/OR structure. Since information elicitation for selecting the PER has already been done, the question arises as to whether there is now any point in carrying out information elicitation again.

It is important to note that the concern of the decision-maker now is different. When doing PER selection, the decision-maker looks at macro-level issues, what are the possible rules that can be applied and which one is the best suited for the situation at hand. However, after this is done, the concern of the decision-maker shifts to the issue of how the action of the selected PER shall be carried out. This change in viewpoint suggests that the information elicited now shall be different from that elicited earlier.

Table 5.7 Early information for action "Re-designate x"

Elicitation method			Information base				
			Entity	Attribute	History	Category	Function
CSFI	Patient satisfaction		Patient		Yearly		Count
ENDSI	*Ends*	*Effectiveness*	Lab test	Cost			Sum
	Maximize economic return	Revenue generated	Doctor	Salary			Sum
				Consultancy fee			Sum
			Nurse	Salary			Sum
				Service fee			Sum
MEANSI	*Means*	*Efficiency*	Hospital	Specialty		Type	Count
	Select another specialty	Expertise needed	Patients	Name			Count
			Disease	Specialty		Type	Count
			Doctors	Qualification			Count
			Nurses				Count
			Equipment				Count
	Become general hospital	Expertise needed	Patients	Name		Type	Count
			Disease	Name		Type	Count
			Equipment	Name			Count

To illustrate consider the PERs as follows. In these rules, priv refers to private rooms. The rules are triggered when a new private room is to be created. If the area of a currently available private room is less than 200, then the first two rules ask for rebuilding it and expanding it, respectively. The third rule is for the case where the area is greater than required, in which case the action is to partition the private room.

(a) WHEN create *priv*IF LT(area(*priv*),200) THEN Rebuild *priv*
(b) WHEN create *priv*, IF LT(area(*priv*),200) THEN Expand *priv*
(c) WHEN create *priv*, IF GT(area(*priv*),200) THEN Partition *priv*

Table 5.8 contains the information elicited for PER selection for rule (b). For the Ends, service more patients, information is about the revenue that shall be generated and for this purpose information about patients using the private room and their income bracket is needed; the diseases for which treatment was offered by disease type; and the 1-month history of diseases treated. Similarly, for the means, remodel room, information about the resources to be raised for remodeling, time and cost as shown are needed.

Now, let the second rule be selected after referring to the information available in the data warehouse fragment for the three PERs. Expand *priv* is now processed from the point of view of its implementation. Let Expand *priv* be atomic; it has no AND/OR decomposition.

Information required to commit to it for operationalization is shown in Table 5.9. Now concern in ENDSI is about the increased capacity that shall be created. For this, history of the daily influx of patients in the ward is required. The new capacity to be created must be compared with the needed capacity to generate the needed revenues and justify the decision. Similarly, in MEANSI, details of the

Table 5.8 Elicited information for selecting PER for Expand *priv*

Elicitation method			Information base				
			Entity	Attribute	History	Category	Function
ENDS I	*Ends*	*Effectiveness*					
	Service more patients	Revenue generated	Patient	Income			Count
			Disease	Name	Month	Type	
MEANSI	*Means*	*Efficiency*					
	Remodel room	Resources needed	Private room	Build time			
				Build cost			
				Rental cost			
				Space			
				Labor cost			

Table 5.9 Elicited information selecting for Expand *priv*

Elicitation method			Information base				
			Entity	Attribute	History	Category	Function
ENDS I	*Ends*	*Effectiveness*					
	Service more patients	Capacity	Patients		Annual	Daily	Count
MEANSI	*Means*	*Efficiency*					
	Construct	Cost	Private room	Cost per sq. metre			Sum
	Break barrier	Cost		Breaking cost per sq. metre			

remodeling to be carried out are needed. The costs of constructing new walls and breaking any existing barriers need to be factored into the decision-making process. Therefore, information for this is relevant and is to be kept in the data warehouse fragment.

We notice that information in Tables 5.8 and 5.9 differ in the level of detail required to finally select the action, Expand *priv*. The Ends for both the tables is the same, "Service more patients". However, the effectiveness measure is different with "revenue generated" at the PER level and "capacity of patients" at the operational level. Similarly, whereas means at the PER level is "Remodel room" with efficiency measure as resources needed in Table 5.8, in Table 5.9 MEANS are "Construct barrier" and "Break barrier".

Even though the level of detail at which information is elicited is different in the two situations, the application of the techniques, the guidance provided, the nature of information model, etc. remain the same.

Complex

If the action of the selected PER in step 1 of the operational decision-making process can be decomposed into AND/OR hierarchy, then in the second step, the decision-maker has to deal with a complex action.

Since during operational decision-making, it is possible that any of AND or OR branch may be selected, the information elicitation process must be applied to all nodes in the AND/OR hierarchy. Consider once again that rule (b) has been selected and it is now required to carry out the second step of the operational decision-making process. Further, Expand *priv* is now a complex action consisting of two sub-actions, Remodel *priv* and Extend *priv*, as shown in Fig. 5.9. Let these be in an OR relationship with each other.

The information to be elicited for Expand *priv* is now that for Remodel *priv* and Extend *priv* respectively. Again the process to be followed in carrying out information elicitation is the same as before. Again, the elicited information may be quite different for the two components of Expand *priv*.

Fig. 5.9 Complex Expand
priv

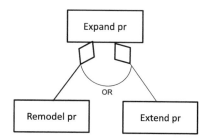

5.9   The Late Information Substage

The late information substage defined in Table 5.2 takes early information as input and produces the ER schema as output. Let us consider the three types of decision-making, policy formulation, PER formulation, and operational decision-making from the perspective of building ER diagrams.

5.9.1   ER Schema for Policy Formulation

In doing information elicitation for policy formulation, the requirements engineer exploits early information obtained by the elicitation techniques.

Additionally, since policies are expressed in the first-order logic, the engineer needs to take into account the main assumption that *simple variables that are quantified refer to entities* and *complex variables that are quantified refer to collections of entities*. Therefore, entities must be created in the ER schema for quantified variables.

Consider the policies as follows:

(a) $\forall x$ [nurse(x) AND GEQ(salary(x), 15000) $\rightarrow$ PFmember(x)]

and

(b) $\forall x \exists B$ [spw(x) AND bed(B) $\rightarrow$ EQ(count(B),2) AND EQ(area(x),200) AND belongs(x, B)]

Policy (a) is built using the simple quantified variable x and it refers to a nurse. This suggests that nurse should be an entity in the ER schema to be built. Policy (b) has two quantified variables, x that refers to spw (semi-private ward) and B to a collection of beds. There must be two entities in the ER schema, one for spw and one for beds.

5.9.2 ER Schema for PER Formulation and Operations

Information elicited for PER formulation, even though it is not based on the elicitation techniques introduced in Sect. 5.4, is in accordance with the early information model of this chapter. Construction of the ER schema is done following the guidelines of the next section.

In contrast, information elicited for operational decision-making is from our four elicitation techniques in accordance with the information model. Therefore, yet again, the guidelines of the next section can be followed to build the ER schema.

5.9.3 Guidelines for Constructing ER Schema

The first step is to resolve any naming conflicts that might arise. It is necessary to ensure, for example, that doctor of CSFI elicitation and doctor of ENDSI elicitation are the same. If this is not the case, then the requirements engineer needs to resolve the conflicting names and find an agreed name for the concept.

Assuming that name conflicts have been resolved, the requirements engineer now picks up the entities and their attributes from the elicited early information. If history is required, then additional attributes to hold it are defined in the entity.

Categorization is handled in two ways. The first is to define an attribute of the entity being categorized, for example, when categorizing disease by its type, we can introduce an attribute, type, in the entity disease. The second is by defining an entity for each different category. A relationship is then set up with this entity and the entity to be categorized. For example, if patients are to be categorized by disease type, then two entity types, patient and disease, are defined. A relationship is then set up between these two.

Finally, functions needed may be handled either dynamically and computed as and when needed, or their values may be pre-computed and stored as derived attributes of entities. In the former case, functions are annotations to indicate that they have to be computed.

The foregoing does not uniformly identify the relationships between the entities of the ER schema. The requirements engineer needs to elicit these from stakeholders during interaction.

We illustrate the use of these guidelines in the construction of the ER schema for the information elicited in Table 5.8. Applying the guidelines, we obtain three entities of the ER schema, namely, Patient, Disease, and Private Room. We introduce the attribute type as shown in Fig. 5.10 for categorizing Disease. Further, as shown Name and Income are attributes of Disease and Patient, respectively. The attributes of Private Room are obtained directly from the attributes found in early information as elicited. These are shown in the ER schema in Fig. 5.10.

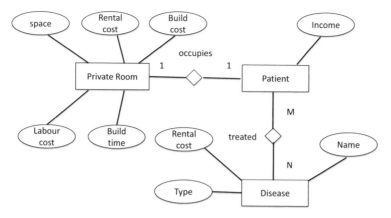

Fig. 5.10 ER schema

The ER schema shows the relationship occupies between Private Room and Patient. This relationship is obtained from the stakeholder during requirements engineer–stakeholder interaction.

5.10   Computer-Based Support for Information Elicitation

We have already indicated the broad nature of Fetchit, the computer-aided requirements engineering tool for data warehouse requirements engineering. The architecture of this tool was introduced in Chap. 4 and is reproduced here in Fig. 5.11, for ease of reading.

As already indicated, the early information elicitor is the component of Fetchit that is responsible for obtaining information for the formulated decisions. The user interfaces of three out of the main four components of Fetchit were outlined in Chap. 4. Now, it remains for us to consider the user interfaces of the elicitor.

5.10.1   User Interfaces

There are four user interfaces corresponding to the four methods of information elicitation. We consider each of these in turn.

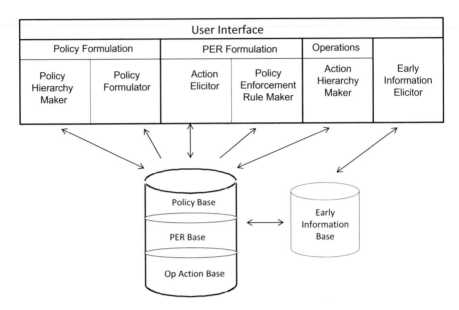

Fig. 5.11 Architecture of Fetchit

CSFI Analysis

Consider the action "start *y*", where y is an instance of OPD. One CSF is to provide quality care. Information needed to estimate this factor is as follows:

- Count of doctor and their specialization,
- Count of patients,
- Disease type, and
- Disease name.

Following our rules, Doctor, Patient, and Disease become entities. Specialization becomes an attribute of the entity Doctor. For the entity Disease, the attribute is the name of the disease. Disease is categorized type-wise.

The user interface for CSFI analysis is shown in Fig. 5.12. The top of the figure shows the action for which information is being elicited and its relevant range variables. The requirements engineer can choose to either select an existing CSF or to create a new one.

Upon selecting the former, a list of the existing CSFs is displayed and the desired CSF can be identified for modification. The latter option is for creating a new CSF and the figure shows the provision made for this. All relevant information about entity, attribute, etc. are also entered in the places provided.

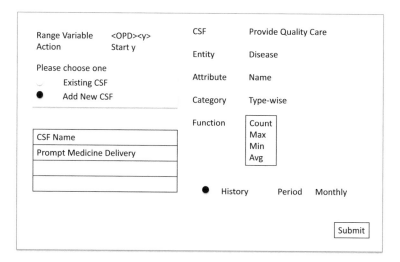

Fig. 5.12   Eliciting information by CSFI analysis

ENDSI Analysis

Consider once again the action "start *y*". Its end is to treat patients using the traditional system of medicine, AYUSH. The effectiveness of this end is measured by the variable patient capacity. An indication of effectiveness can be obtained by keeping information about the patients serviced every day.

The user interface for ENDSI is as shown in Fig. 5.13.

The top of the figure shows the action for which information is being elicited. Again, we have the two options for selecting an already existing End or creating a new End. The former shows a list of existing Ends. For the latter, Ends as well as the effectiveness measure is entered. As before, entity, attribute, etc. are all entered.

MEANSI Analysis

Again consider the action "start *y*" that can be performed by constructing a new OPD. The efficiency variable is land required.

Figure 5.14 shows the user interface. As can be seen, the figure is similar to the ones for CSFI and ENDSI.

Outcome Feedback

In Fetchit, the requirements engineer can enter the sequence of outcomes constituting the feedback loop. Parameters of outcomes are entered in the screen shown in Fig. 5.15. When the initial decision is reached, then the feedback loop is terminated. The starting decision is not re-entered in the sequence.

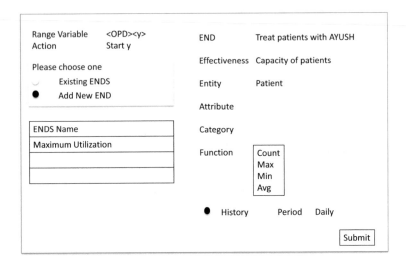

Fig. 5.13 Eliciting information by ENDSI analysis

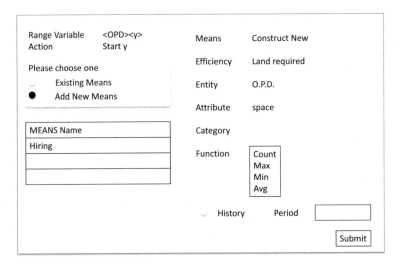

Fig. 5.14 Eliciting information by MEANSI analysis

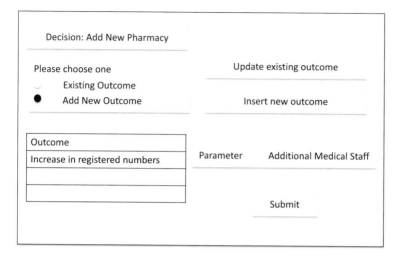

Fig. 5.15 Eliciting parameters through outcome feedback analysis

5.10.2   The Early Information Base

The elicitor of Fetchit interfaces with the early information base as shown in Fig. 5.11. The basic purpose of the information base is to store elicited information. Each piece of elicited information is associated with the decision it is elicited for. It may happen that the same piece of information is elicited for more than one decision. In this case, the information will be associated with each decision separately. Therefore, three bases, the policy base, PER base, and the Op action base, interact with the early information base as shown in Fig. 5.11.

The repository supporting early information elicitor tool is in three parts as shown in Fig. 5.16. The decision base contains the decisions; factor and variables base contains factors and variables; information base contains information resulting from the population of the information model. These three parts are related to one another as shown in the figure.

The repository exploits the relationship between the different bases to provide traceability. Information in the information base can be traced back to its source decision either directly or transitively through factors and variables. It is also possible to retrieve information relevant to given decisions as well as to factors and variables. A query facility exists to support this.

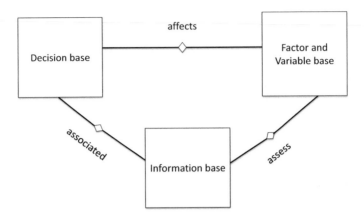

Fig. 5.16 The structure of the repository

5.11   Conclusion

A decision is the crucial concept that gives rise to our approach to data warehouse requirements engineering. We refer to this approach as decisional requirements engineering. The notion of a decision is closely related to the achievement factors, CSF, ENDS, MEANS, and Outcome Feedback. Therefore, in making the decision–achievement factor relationship explicit, we get

- Guidance: All techniques guide the requirements engineering process by introducing factors and variables before determining early information. Further, there is an information model to populate;
- The association decision information, as well as the information factor association; and
- Traceability of information.

The first issue that we addressed is that of creating interest in stakeholders to become active participants in the requirements engineering process in a sustained manner. We achieve this by determining important managerial concerns and developing elicitation techniques for each of these. The second issue is as to identify a range of techniques that are as comprehensive as possible. This reduces the possibility of missing information requirements while doing requirements engineering. We achieve this by developing a suite of techniques to be used collectively.

Requirements engineers emphasize that a consensus on the requirements specification among all stakeholders is crucial. Failing such an agreement, system development may suffer from, for example, conflicting requirements, and wrongly prioritized requirements. This goes well with Sect. 2.6 where five factors that affect alignment of business with the data warehouse were presented.

Conventional wisdom in requirements engineering is that ad hoc interviews without having a model to populate relies overly on the experience of the requirements engineer. Existence of a model makes stakeholders stay focused on the concepts of the model and makes it possible for tool support to be provided. Requirements engineering tools provide several features like keeping the requirements repository, checking model constraints, and providing guidance on what can be done next.

It is assumed that requirements engineering produces complete requirements specifications for the entire development to be carried out. Therefore, requirements engineering is time-consuming, inflexible, and not dynamic enough to deal with dynamically changing requirements, and leads to long lead times to product delivery.

In the next chapter, we consider the issue of agile data warehouse development and the role that agile requirements engineering plays in it.

References

1. Golfarelli, M., Maio, D., & Rizzi, S. (1998, January). Conceptual design of data warehouses from E/R schemes. In *Proceedings of the Thirty-First Hawaii International Conference on System Sciences, 1998* (Vol. 7, pp. 334–343). IEEE.
2. Hüsemann, B., Lechtenbörger, J., & Vossen, G. (2000). Conceptual data warehouse design. In *Proceedings of the International Workshop on Design and Management of Data Warehouses (DMDW2000)*, Stockholm, Sweden.
3. Moody, L. D., & Kortink, M. A. R. (2000). From enterprise models to dimensional models: a methodology for data warehouses and data mart design. In *Proceedings of the International Workshop on Design and Management of Data Warehouses*, Stockholm, Sweden (pp. 5.1–5.12).
4. Prakash, D., & Prakash, N. (to appear). A multi-factor approach for elicitation of information requirements of data warehouses. *Requirements Engineering Journal*.
5. Prakash, N., Prakash, D., & Sharma, Y. K. (2009). Towards better fitting data warehouse systems. In *The practice of enterprise modeling* (pp. 130–144). Berlin Heidelberg: Springer.

Chapter 6
The Development Process

In the last few chapters, we saw that there are three sources of decisions and each source has information associated with it. Thus, the policy formulation layer had policy formulation decisions and early information associated with each decision; the PER formulation layer also had PER formulation decisions and associated information; and the operational decision layer has actions as decisions and similarly its own early information.

In this chapter, we look at the development of our Data Warehouse fragment from an agile point of view. For this, a model-driven technique to arrive at the user stories is discussed. The instantiation of the model gives us a requirements granule. Since the development process is agile, multiple iterations are carried out and multiple requirements granules and therefore multiple DW fragments are obtained.

This means that in fact there is a need for agile development and consolidation to proceed together. This is to remove problems of inconsistency that will arise if there are multiple DW fragments in the enterprise. Thus, this chapter also discusses a five-step process to consolidation. This is a semi-automated process, and our tool Fetchit supports the consolidation process.

6.1 Agile Data Warehouse Development

As discussed in Chaps. 1 and 2, agile techniques like Scrum aim for rapid and piecemeal product delivery where a user story is an identified requirement. It is therefore crucial to write good user stories. However, the essential difficulty in scripting user stories is that it requires highly skilled and experienced project architects/product owners. Consequently, it is ad hoc and experience based. There is a need for making this more systematic and providing better guidance in the task of writing user stories.

© Springer Nature Singapore Pte Ltd. 2018
N. Prakash and D. Prakash, *Data Warehouse Requirements Engineering*,
https://doi.org/10.1007/978-981-10-7019-8_6

"Goodness" of a user story is obtained by (a) "epic–theme–story" decomposition method and (b) INVEST test. Even while applying these, there are three major problem areas:

- The notions of an epic, theme, and user story are based on the fuzzy notion of largeness. Consequently, it is difficult to distinguish between these.
- There are no guidelines on how to decompose epics into themes and themes into stories.
- In applying INVEST to user stories, determining the Small is not apparent.

In order to mitigate these difficulties, we consider, in this chapter, a model-driven approach to arrive at user stories. This approach makes the task of identifying a requirement relatively more precise because

- We now focus on instantiating the model. Thus, the fuzzy notion of largeness is dropped in identifying relevant concepts of the application.
- Guidance is provided by the model in the task of developing user stories.
- The model defines criteria for selecting model components. Other non-model oriented stakeholder concerns are then considered to make the right selection.

For this model-driven approach, the term user story is redefined. Recall from Scrum that a user story provides a sketch of a "feature" that will be of value to a stakeholder. It provides a brief idea about the functionality needed in an application. A user story is expressed in three parts, who, what, and why parts, respectively. The first part identifies the stakeholder, the second the desired action, and the third the reason behind the action.

For the model-driven approach to data warehouse development, the basic structure of a user story is retained but modified for data warehouse development such that

1. "Who": identifies the stakeholder,
2. "What": identifies the needed information, and
3. "Why": identifies the decision that is the reason for the needed information.

We will refer to such a model-driven story as a DW user story to distinguish it from the Scrum story.

Thus, for agile data warehouse development, **a DW user story expresses the information required by a stakeholder for taking a decision**. Interest in agile data warehouse development is in building an initial backlog of DW user stories.

Table 6.1 summarizes the difference between a user story for OLTP systems and that of data warehouse systems.

Table 6.1 Difference between Scrum user story and DW user story

	Scrum user story	DW user story
"Who"	Stakeholder	Stakeholder
"What"	Desired action	Information
"Why"	Reason behind desired action	Decision

6.2   Decision Application Model (DAM) for Agility

The decision application model (DAM), see Fig. 6.1, is the basis for doing model-driven agile data warehouse development.

A decision application (DA) consists of a set of elements about which a decision is to be taken. For example, a DA that

- Formulates policies of an organization has as elements the various policies that need to be accepted, rejected, or modified;
- Decides upon policy enforcement rules of the enterprise has as elements the various business rules of the enterprise; and
- Judges what action is to be taken next has these actions as elements.

Figure 6.1 shows that an element may be simple or complex. A simple element is atomic and cannot be decomposed further, whereas a complex element is built from other elements. Thus, complex business rules of Chap. 4 are built out of simpler business rules connected by logical operators.

There are two kinds of relationships among elements, namely, compatible and conflict. An element may be in conflict with zero or more elements as shown by the cardinalities of conflict. An element is compatible with one or more elements as shown in Fig. 6.1. Let us consider these two relationships in turn.

When an element E_1 is in **conflict** with another element E_2, then the former is achieved at the cost of the latter. This cost may be financial, performance, flexibility, and security. Conflict may also arise due to diverging stakeholder interests, or simply because one element interferes with achievement of others.

Consider two elements as follows:

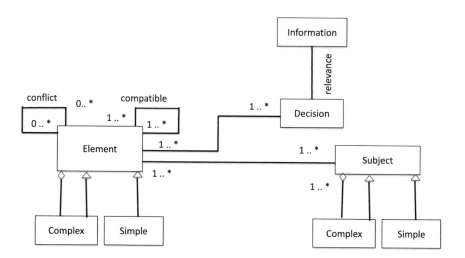

Fig. 6.1 The decision application model

E_1: Give liberal staff benefits
E_2: Ensure high profitability

Both of these are policies of a business house. Since staff benefits come from company profits, the policy element E_1 entails reduction in profits. Therefore, policies represented by E_1 and E_2 are in conflict.

In order to see the occurrence of conflict in business rules, consider the two elements as follows:

E_1': WHEN .... IF stock rupture occurs THEN supply to privileged customers
E_2': WHEN .... IF stock rupture occurs THEN supply only to pending orders

These elements enter into conflict because pending orders may be of non-privileged customers but a new order by a privileged customer may have just arrived.

It can be seen that conflict has the properties as follows:

- Anti-reflexive: E is not in conflict with itself.
- Symmetric: If E_1 is in conflict with E_2, then E_2 is in conflict with E_1.
- Anti-transitive: IF E_1 conflicts E_2 and E_2 conflicts E_3, then we cannot conclude that E_1 conflicts E_3.

We consider an element E_1 to be **compatible** with another element E_2 if it promotes the latter. As before, this promotion can be in financial terms or in the form of performance, security, or convergence of stakeholder concerns.

Consider the two policies as follows:

E_2: Ensure high profitability
E_3: Increase market share

These are compatible because they promote one another.
Similarly, we can see that the two enforcement rules are compatible:

E_4': WHEN .... IF stock rupture occurs THEN reduce supply
E_1': WHEN .... IF stock rupture occurs THEN supply to privileged customers only

Compatibility displays properties as follows:

- Reflexive: element E is compatible with itself.
- Symmetric: If element E_1 is compatible with element E_2, then E_2 is compatible with E_1.
- Anti-transitive: IF element E_1 is compatible with element E_2 and E_2 is compatible with element E_3, then we cannot conclude that E_1 is compatible with E_3.

Note that elements may be independent, that is, they may not be compatible or in conflict with others. Thus, for example the two elements as follows are independent:

E_4': WHEN .... IF stock rupture occurs THEN reduce supply
E_5: WHEN .... IF stock rupture occurs THEN replenish stock

As shown in Fig. 6.1, an element is associated with a subject. A subject itself may be simple or complex. A simple subject is atomic and cannot be decomposed into simpler ones, whereas a complex subject is constructed out of other subjects. For example, Salesperson Deployment is a simple subject, whereas Marketing is a complex subject composed of the subjects Salesperson Deployment, Sales, Inventory, and Branding.

The subject of a DA identifies the major concerns of the application. For example, a policy enforcement rules DA that is for salesperson deployment has as its elements those rules that are relevant to salesperson deployment. When the DA is about optimizing salesperson deployment, then the application consists of the set of actions for doing so.

A DA may itself be simple or complex. This is because a complex DA can be decomposed into its sub-applications subject-wise. In our example, there is a simple DA for Salesperson Deployment. When composed together with the Sales, Inventory, and Branding DA, it forms the complex DA, Marketing.

Figure 6.1 shows the relationship between an element and decisions of interest. These decisions are represented in a choice set associated with the element. Broadly speaking, these decisions are to select the element, reject it, or to modify it. This is in accordance with the decisions of Chap. 4.

A member of the choice set, a decision, may itself be simple or complex. In the latter case, the member has its own choice set and this gives rise to a decision hierarchy. Chapter 5 discusses this in detail and so it is not elaborated here. A member that has no choice set is said to be simple.

Finally, Fig. 6.1 shows that a decision is associated with the information that is relevant to it. By relevance, we mean that selection, rejection, or modification is facilitated by consulting of the associated information. Recall that Data Warehouse requirements engineering techniques obtain information in several forms as follows:

(a) Early information,
(b) An ER diagram, and
(c) Facts and dimensions.

Since DW user stories aim only for enough information to proceed to the development stage, from the point of view of being agile, **it is adequate to obtain information in early information form**. Of course, information will have to be structured but in agile development this would be done after building the backlog of user stories.

6.3 A Hierarchical View

DAM suggests a hierarchy of concerns. The topmost level is the application level. It deals with elements and their properties, namely, simple/complex and compatible/conflict, respectively.

The application level is populated as an undirected graph with nodes as elements and two types of edges to represent the relationships. These relationships are compatible and conflict. Compatibility relationship between nodes is represented as a solid line, whereas the conflicting relationship is represented as a dashed line.

Recall that the relationship compatible is reflexive. Therefore, there should be a self-loop on each element of the element graph because every element is compatible with itself. We do not explicitly represent such self-loops in the graph to avoid unnecessary cluttering.

Figure 6.2 shows the graph for the elements E_1', E_2', and E_4' considered in Sect. 6.2.

The second level of concern is the decision level. In contrast to the application level, the decision level is populated with decisions that are of relevance in the organization. It considers each node of the element graph as a candidate for selection, rejection, and modification. Consequently, each element gives rise to three alternatives and the decision level shown in Fig. 6.2 (that contains three elements) is populated by nine decisions. However, this is a top-level view because as already discussed, each decision may itself be complex giving rise to a decision hierarchy. It is assumed that there are no cycles in this hierarchy. **The decision level is populated by the choice set of decisions and the decision hierarchy in the case of complex decisions**.

The third level of concern is the information level. By identifying the set of decisions of interest in a decision application, the second level acts as a bridge between the decision application and the information relevant for taking decisions. This latter aspect lies in the area of the information level. The information level is populated by early information required to decide on whether to select, reject, or modify an element. Thus, for each choice set in the decision level, there is information in the information level.

Figure 6.3 shows an example of the three levels with the application level instantiated with elements, the decision level with the choice set of decisions, and the information level with information for making a selection from each choice set. Notice, in the application level, that the figure shows elements E_6 to E_{12} that are independent and not in any relationship with each other.

Now, each level of the instance diagram provides a definition of the notion of a requirement. This is summarized in Table 6.2.

From the point of view of the application level, the requirements engineering interest is to identify the constituent elements of the decision application and the inter-relationships between these. This gives us the view of **a requirement as the elements about which decisions are to be taken** or more specifically, in terms of DAM, the elements, and their compatible/conflicting elements. Notice that this is concerned with strategic business requirements.

Focus at the decision level is to identify the set of decisions that meet business needs as stated in the application level and, thereafter, to select that subset which is

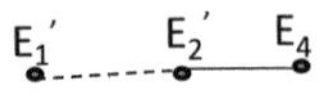

Fig. 6.2 The element graph

$$E_1' \text{ } \text{-}\text{-}\text{-}\text{-}\text{-} \text{ } E_2' \text{ } E_4'$$

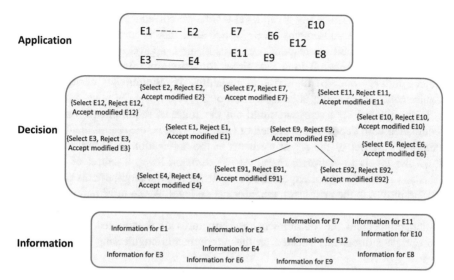

Fig. 6.3 The three levels of the decision application model

Table 6.2 The changing notion of requirements

Level	Definition of requirement
Application	The elements together with their compatible/conflicting elements
Decision	The backlog of decisions that meet the business strategic requirement
Information	The information relevant to each decision of the decision application

to be taken into the development run. It can be inferred **that a requirement at this level is the backlog of decisions that meet the business strategic requirement**. Clearly, the decision level is concerned with the tactics to be adopted in the business to deliver the identified strategy.

At the information level, we get information requirement. We see that the structure of the information is treated as relatively unimportant. Rather, it is important to establish a relationship between the elicited, relatively unstructured information, and a decision at the decision level. Thus, **a requirement here is the information relevant to each decision of the decision application**.

6.4   Granularity of Requirements

It is clear that the DAM model gives a stack of requirements. Now, there are two ways to do DWRE. One approach is to slice the stack horizontally and process a level completely before moving to the next one. In other words, we look at requirements level-wise where requirements engineering yields the totality of requirements granules at any given level before we consider requirements from the perspective of the subsequent level. Notice that this is in accordance with the waterfall model and corresponds to breadth-first approach of Chap. 2. This approach suffers from (a) long lead times for delivering requirements as well as project delivery and (b) high risk of instability if requirements change even as requirements engineering is being carried out.

In the second approach, we could cut the stack of requirements vertically, in accordance with depth-first approach of Chap. 2. That is, the requirements engineer identifies a subset of the set of elements at the application level and then moves down the levels to elaborate these. At the decision level, a subset of elaborated decisions is picked up for exploring. From decisions, the requirements engineering process moves to the next level, the information level. Again information elicitation is followed by selection of a subset of this information. From this selected information, conceptual and multidimensional structures are determined. To summarize, appropriate subsets are selected as the requirements engineering process moves vertically down.

Let us take a detailed look at the second approach. The top left corner of Fig. 6.4 shows requirements engineering is at the application level where elements and the relationships between these elements are being discovered. Now, even as new elements are being discovered, the requirements engineer selects E_1, E_2, E_3, E_4, E_9, and E_{10} (marked in green) to be taken for elaboration to the decision level, leaving out E_7 and E_8 (marked in red) for the time being. Notice that requirements engineering is now being performed at two levels, at the application level where even more elements are being discovered and at the decision level where decisions and decision hierarchies are being obtained for the selected elements.

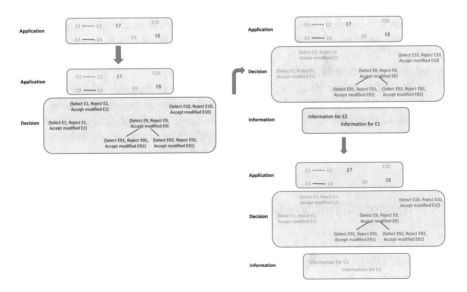

Fig. 6.4 Bringing agility to the three levels of DAM

The bottom left corner of Fig. 6.4 shows population of the decision level for E_1, E_2, E_9, and E_{10}. The choice set of decisions for E_9 is complex and so a decision hierarchy is obtained. Decisions for elements E_3 and E_4 are yet to be discovered.

The requirements engineer may now decide that information to take a decision on E_1 and E_2 is required and so, as shown in the top right corner of the figure, the choice set of decisions for E_1 and E_2 are marked in green and taken down to the information level. Notice again that requirements engineering is now being performed at the application and decision levels where even more elements and even more decisions are being discovered, and also at the information level where information for E_1 and E_2 is being elicited.

Finally, the requirements engineer may either decide that information of both E_1 and E_2 may go to the conceptual and construction phase, or alternatively, s/he may choose one of the two. At this point we can now define a **requirements granule as the selected subset of information**. Thus, for the former case, where information for both E_1 and E_2 is selected, the requirements granule consists of information of E_1 and E_2. While with the latter, the requirements granule will only contain the information of say, E_1.

The bottom right side of the figure shows the selection of both information of E_1 and E_2 (marked in green). This requirements granule is taken down into the conceptual design and the construction phase giving us a DW fragment. In this case, the DW fragment addresses decisions for elements E_1 and E_2.

This selection makes up a single iteration of agile DWRE. Let us say we just performed iteration 1.

There are several starting points for iteration 2. Recall that out of the selected elements at the application level, decisions for E_3 and E_4 were not elaborated in iteration 1. Thus, one starting point for iteration 2 is at the decision level where again it may be decided that either decisions for both E_3 and E_4 will be looked at or only one will be looked at. This iteration will proceed to the information level where a selection will produce a requirements granule that will be taken into development.

Another starting point for iteration 2 is at the application level where elements not selected in any previous iteration are up for selection. The process moves down the sub-levels as discussed in iteration 1.

It follows that there is in fact a third starting point for iteration 2, at the information level. Here, a selection is made from previously unselected information and the requirements granule is arrived at. Thus, *subsequent iterations can in fact begin at any level of our stack of requirements*.

Notice that the size of the DW fragment depends on the size of the requirements granule. In other words, if information for a large number of elements is selected for a given iteration, then the DW fragment will also be large.

This strategy is similar to the epic–theme–story strategy of Scrum. In Scrum, the epics are obtained and reduced to yield themes from which stories are obtained. This reduction operation yields stories and stories meeting the INVEST test are taken up for development.

Note carefully that the three levels, application, decision, and information, do NOT correspond to epic, theme, and story, respectively. In fact, these levels reduce the fuzziness associated with the ideas of epic, theme, and user story, by using relatively concrete notions of (a) concepts for which decisions are taken, (b) the decisions, and (c) the information relevant to the decisions.

In the development process, vertical slices of requirements to be elaborated are selected. The full specification is obtained only at the end of the project.

6.4.1   Selecting the Right Granularity

Evidently, there is a trade-off between thickness and lead times to project delivery. Therefore, agility is promoted when computer-based support is provided for low thickness vertical slices. Maximum lead time occurs when the entire element graph and the complete decision hierarchy constitute the vertical slice. We will consider the issue of thickness at the three levels separately.

Application Level

First notice that there are two drives that can lead to initial identification of elements:

- The subject drive: Stakeholder identifies a subject of interest and the elements of interest are elicited.
- The element drive: The stakeholder directly identifies elements independent of any subject. The subject, if any, is identified only after element identification is done.

Irrespective of the drive, the vertical slice to be taken up for development must be determined. There are three factors to be considered. These are as follows:

Factor I: Topological

We view this in terms of the element graph. An element graph has the following:

- An **isolated** node: Such a node has no edges. That is, such a node does not conflict with any other and is also not compatible with any other node (note: but by reflexivity, it is compatible only with itself).
- A **node cluster** for a node N comprises N and all nodes with which N is connected by *compatible* or *conflict* edges.

From the element graph, a number of candidate elements for selection can be identified. A single-node cluster, for example, is a candidate. In Fig. 6.5, consider node cluster C_2 for node E_6. E_6 is compatible with E_2 and in conflict with E_4. Thus, the node cluster for E_6 comprises E_2 and E_4.

We can also build slices that span across multiple node clusters. If node A belongs to the node cluster of N, then we can consider the cluster formed by A in our slice as well. Such a cluster consists of nodes directly connected to N, and also

Fig. 6.5 Defining thickness of a cluster

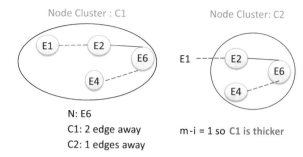

of those indirectly connected to N by being two edges away (by being connected to A). This can be extended to include nodes three edges away, four edges away, and in general k edges away. Consider node cluster C_1 shown in Fig. 6.5. Here, while considering the slice, node E_1 which is in conflict with E_2 is also considered in the cluster of E_6. In fact, E_1 is a node that is two edges away from E_6. Nodes E_2 and E_4 are directly connected to E_6 or one edge away.

We can now define the notion of thickness of a node cluster. Consider two node clusters C_1 and C_2 for the node N. C_1 is thicker than C_2 if one of the following holds:

- C_1 comprises nodes m edges away from N, whereas C_2 comprises nodes $(m - i)$, $i \geq 1$, edges away from N. In Fig. 6.5, node cluster C_1 has E_1 that is two edges away from E_6 and so m = 2. Node cluster C_2 has all directly connected nodes to E_6 and so i = 1. Since $(m - i) = 1$, node cluster C_1 is thicker than C_2.
- C_1 and C_2 both comprise nodes that are m edges away from N but the number of nodes in the former is greater than in the latter. In other words, if a node cluster is more heavily populated than another, then it is thicker than the latter. Consider the two node clusters in Fig. 6.6. Both C_1 and C_2 have nodes directly connected to E_6. However, in C_1 the slice includes E_7, E_2, and E_4 and slice C_2 picks E_2 and E_4. Since C_1 has three nodes that are directly connected to E_6 compared with two in cluster C_2, C_1 is thicker than C_2.

Fig. 6.6 Thickness of node clusters where both clusters have nodes m edges away

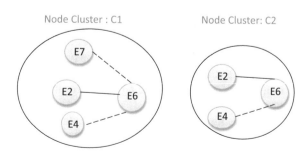

The notion of thickness suggests that at the application level isolated nodes are the best slices. Thereafter, less thick node clusters as per the criteria outlined above are next best slices.

Whereas the foregoing provides a syntactic view of the thickness of a slice, it is possible to bring in semantics as well. There are two semantic criteria as follows.

Factor II: Business Coherence

The notion of coherence can be used to reduce the thickness of slices. If nodes of a candidate are strongly related, then the requirements engineer needs to investigate whether the entire candidate is to be selected or whether it is possible to select a suitable subset of it.

Coherence is defined on the basis of the shared properties of nodes. That is, a set of nodes, S, is coherent if each member of the set has the same property P with respect to a certain designated member of S. There are three properties of interest, Compatible, Conflict, and Compatible OR Conflict.

Evidently, an isolated node is coherent under compatibility. This is because compatibility is reflexive. Therefore, it remains the most preferred candidate even under business coherence.

There are three possibilities for a node cluster of N as follows:

(a) The entire node cluster is coherent since every node in it satisfies the property Compatible OR Conflict with respect to the node N.
(b) The subset of the node cluster formed from conflicting nodes only is coherent. This is because the property Conflict is satisfied by all nodes in the cluster with respect to N.
(c) The subset of the node cluster formed compatible nodes only is also coherent. This is because the property, Compatible, is satisfied by all nodes in the cluster with respect to N.

Evidently, both node clusters (b) and (c) are thinner than the node cluster (a). This is because they are less heavily populated, that is, they contain a lesser number of nodes that the node cluster (a). When a choice is to be made between node clusters (b) and (c), then this can be done by determining their populations and the cluster with lesser number of nodes can be selected.

Factor III: Business Priority

Whereas topological and coherence considerations are derived from the element graph, it possible that there are other stakeholder concerns that influence the choice of elements to be taken up. This may happen if selection of an element could result in financial benefits, performance efficiencies, security, etc. Thus, business priority plays a role in selecting the element to be taken up for data warehouse support.

However, topology and coherence produce a menu of choices from which the ones with higher priority could be picked up.

Decision Level

Whereas the application level provides the strategic business view, **the decision level provides the "Why" component of our user story**.

There are two essential questions to be answered at the decision level:

1. How do we construct decisions from the selected elements?
2. How do we select the vertical slice of the decision level that will be taken into the information level?

Regarding the first question, the set of alternatives is available in the choice sets that result from entities. We postulate that for a given element E, the interesting choice set is {Select E, Reject E, and Accept modified E}. In other words, if an element is a policy, a business rule, or an action then the policy, business rule, or action, respectively, may be selected, rejected, or accepted after some modification. Applying this to all elements, we get as many choice sets as the number of elements handed down by the application level.

Recall from Fig. 6.1 that elements may be simple or complex. For complex elements, every component E_i of the element itself participates in the choice set {Select E_i, Reject E_i, and Accept modified E_i}.

Now, let us consider the second question, namely, that of selecting decisions for determining the thickness of the vertical slice. Recall that decisions are organized in a hierarchy. Selection therefore amounts to selecting the appropriate branch of the hierarchy. There are several selection criteria as follows:

Feasibility: The first selection criterion is whether a decision lying on a branch is feasible or not. A feasible decision is that which can be considered for implementation, whereas a non-feasible decision is one that cannot be implemented in a given situation in the business. Clearly, only feasible decisions are candidates for selection.

Frequency: If an alternative is likely to be implemented with high frequency, then it is a good candidate for data warehouse support. Consider an alternative Select Replenish Stock. If this decision is to be taken with high frequency, then data warehouse support would be a good idea. Similarly, frequency of Reject Replenish Stock has a bearing on whether a data warehouse will be built or not.

Bottleneck: When delays occur for reasons like the absence of defined policies, business rules, or unknown next action to be taken, then data warehouse support would be helpful. This is because such delays in turn call for formulation/reformulation of a policy, a business rule, or for identifying the next action to be taken. Thus, if the decision to replenish stock causes such delay and is a bottleneck, then Select Replenish Stock is a good candidate for providing data warehouse support.

Performance: Alternatives that contribute toward organizational efficiency and/or effectiveness are clearly good candidates for providing DW support.

Applying these criteria yields a subset of the set of constructed alternatives. This subset is now to be taken explored from the point of view of the relevant information.

Information Level

For completing our user story, we need to associate with a decision, the information relevant to it to **provide the "What" of the user story**. The purpose of the information level is to identify this information.

The starting point for identifying information is a selected decision. This information is obtained as "early" by deploying CSFI, ENDSI, MEANSI, and outcome feedback techniques described in Chap. 5.

Semantic criteria are deployed here for selection of information that is to form the requirements granule. These include priority. Information with higher priority will be selected over information with lower priority. Another semantic criterion is bottleneck. This is similar to the bottleneck described above for selecting decisions.

Once the requirements granule is formed, development of the DW fragment proceeds through the conceptual and remaining phases of DW life cycle.

6.5 Showing Agility Using an Example

Subject of the decision application: Leave policy formulation of a Hospital
"Who" of user story: Deputy Director (HR)

Consider the policies
P_1: Give compensatory off to doctors working on any National Holiday.
P_2: In case of an outbreak, suspend leave of all doctors and nursing staff.
P_3: All employees can avail a maximum of 8 casual leaves in a year.
P_4: In case a holiday falls on a Monday or on a Friday, then that Monday or Friday will be made a working day.
P_5: At any time the hospital should have at least one consultant from each unit on 24 h duty.

Let us instantiate the three levels of DAM. The application level is populated with policies as elements along with relationship between them. Policy P_2 is in conflict with P_1 and P_3. Further, P_4 and P_5 are isolated nodes. The element graph is as shown in Fig. 6.7.

Let us now apply the three criteria relevant to the application level.

Fig. 6.7 Element graph for policies

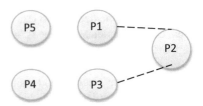

Topological: There are several node clusters that are possible. One node cluster is for node P_2 with P_1 and P_3 as directly connected nodes. Let us call this C_1. Another node cluster can be C_1 along with node P_4. Let us call this C_2. When comparing C_1 and C_2, we find that C_1 is thinner than C_2 as C_1 has lesser number of nodes than C_2. Similarly, C_3 cluster contains nodes of C_1 and node P_5. Again C_1 is thinner. Consider yet another cluster that contains all the nodes of the element graph. This naturally is the thickest cluster. Finally, there are two more possibilities, namely the clusters that contain only the isolated nodes. These naturally are the thinnest clusters.

Business coherence: node cluster of P_2 containing P_2, P_1 and P_3 are coherent since all the nodes are in a conflicting relationship. So this is a good candidate to select.

Business priority: Let us say that policy P_5 is given highest priority and is decided to be implemented first. Policy P_3 is given second highest priority.

Now, the requirements engineer has a choice to make since the two criteria for selecting the slice give different nodes to select. Since stakeholder priority is important, s/he decides that policy P_5 will be selected in the first iteration. Thus, P_5 goes down to the decision level to be elaborated.

Decision level: Policy P_5 at the decision level is converted into a decision hierarchy based on the process described in Chap. 4. Here, the policy is expressed in the logic form and a structural hierarchy tree is constructed. With each node of the hierarchy, a choice set {select, modify, reject} is attached. This forms the decision level.

Now, applying criteria namely feasibility, frequency, bottleneck, and performance decisions to be elaborated at the information level are selected. Suppose two nodes selected be "consultant" and "duty must be 24 h".

Information level: Applying CSFI, ENDSI, MEANSI, and outcome feedback early information is elicited. A subset of this information is to be selected to form the requirements granule. Assume all the elicited information is selected.

We can now construct our DW user stories. Each row of Table 6.3 constitutes a DW user story. This backlog is now available to development teams to take into data warehouse development.

Table 6.3 Forming the initial backlog of DW user stories

Decision (WHY)	Information (WHAT)
Select consultant	Specialty of consultant
	Average experience of consultants
	Maximum qualification of consultants unit-wise
Select duty must be 24 h	Unit-wise name of consultant on duty
	Total number of consultants on 24 h duty

6.6 Comparison of DAM and Epic–Theme–Story Approach

The differences between DAM approach of arriving at the user story and epic–theme–story approach is summarized in Table 6.4. The comparison has been done along various aspects and is the first column of the table. The second column of the table displays the lessons learnt in applying the epic–theme–story approach. The third column lists the way DAM deals with these aspects.

The first row of the table considers the speed of progress in the user story writing against the level of detail that is to be reached. The risk in stakeholder interaction is that the discussion can go into details of business processes, information life cycles, and data transformation rules. It is necessary to avoid this kind of detail so that the task of story writing proceeds at a good pace. In the DAM approach, elaboration of the element graph, element reduction, and the decision hierarchy are the crucial structures. It is important to limit the element graph to consider nodes directly connected to a node; otherwise, the spread becomes too large. Element reduction and construction of the decision hierarchy need to be taken into detail. The finer the detail, the more specific is the user story that shall emerge.

The second row contains recommendations about how to keep the interaction short. In column two of this row, we see the importance of staying at the business level, i.e., to deal with measures and qualifiers. In our case, the focus is to consider the full range in which early information can be expressed.

According to the third row, there is a difference between when the story is discovered. The epic–theme–story approach with its focus on dashboards detects user stories when stakeholders talk about what they will do with the dashboards

Table 6.4 Lessons learnt

Aspect	Epic–theme–story of Scrum	Decision application model
Level of detail versus speed	Project architect must maintain a balance	Elaboration of element graph, element reduction, and decision hierarchy
Interview level	Stay at business level	Stay with early information
User Story detection	When stakeholders say what they do	Upon decision selection
Focus	Focus is on the "what" of user story	Balance the focus on "why" and "what" of user stories
Prioritizing user stories	At epic and theme level	At three levels namely element graph, element reduction, and decision hierarchy
Story management	Manual	Computer-assisted
Business target model	Developed even as a story is developed	No target model Concentrate on stories, business target model is a consequence of early information

once the data identified in the theme is in place. On the other hand, a DW user story is detected the moment the decision is selected for taking into development.

The fourth row says that our model-driven approach balances the why and what aspects of the user story. In the epic–theme approach, the why and who aspects remain static over a long period of time. Focus is on the changing what aspect of a story. There is need for reinforcement that interview is still about the same why.

From the point of view of managing stories and their components, the model-driven approach is computer supported. Element graphs, element reduction, and decision hierarchies are all stored in the repository of our tool. Information elicited for each decision–information association is also kept in the tool repository.

Lastly, there is a clear attempt at building the target business model in the epic-theme approach. This is done even as the stakeholder interaction is being carried out. The measures and qualifiers are laid out in what is essentially a multidimensional form. Simultaneously, epics, themes, and stories are being detected. This overloading of the project architect is avoided in the model-driven approach where a separation of concerns occurs due to the application, decision, and information levels.

6.7 Data Warehouse Consolidation

Figure 6.8 shows that DW fragments may arise at any of policy formulation, PER formulation, and operational levels. This is as a consequence of requirements granules populating these levels. Two cases arise:

A. DW fragment development of each level of decision-making is done level-wise with policy DW developed first followed by PER DW followed by operational DW. Here, the requirements granules produced at any time will belong to the same level or are **horizontal** with respect to the other.
B. DW fragment development does not proceed level-wise but vertically across levels. Thus, for certain policies formulated, the requirements engineer may proceed to formulate enforcement rules for these policies and finally operational

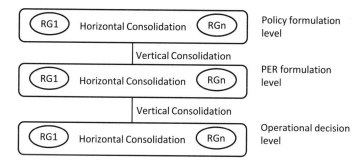

Fig. 6.8 Horizontal and vertical integration

decisions may be formulated. Here, the requirements granules produced are from different levels or are **vertical** with respect to the other.

The foregoing suggests that data warehouse consolidation is needed for both horizontally and vertically related DW fragments. Thus, we have two kinds of consolidation, horizontal consolidation and vertical consolidation. Let us consider these in turn.

Horizontal consolidation: This refers to integrating requirements granules at the same level. Consider the operational level (Fig. 6.8) consisting of data warehouse fragments for supporting operational decision-making. Since all the requirements granules are at the operational level, their consolidation is referred to as horizontal consolidation. Similarly, horizontal consolidation is shown at the policy formulation and PER formulation levels.

Vertical Consolidation: The need for vertical consolidation arises because of the continuum between the three levels of decision-making. Recall that this continuum says that (a) the three DW fragments operate in the same decision environment and (b) there is a relationship between them: the policy level provides the rationale for the PER level and the PER level provides rationale for the operational level. In vertical consolidation, requirements granules that are consolidated are from different decision levels.

Recall that need for consolidation in data warehouses arises due to the desirability of having a common data model as well as a common platform. In the absence of the former, the well-known problem of inconsistency is faced at the operational level. That is, whereas the presence of inconsistency has been shown in the horizontal dimension, it has yet to be shown that inconsistencies can arise in the vertical dimension. The harmful effects of this inconsistency are also to be demonstrated.

We show that information can be common across requirements granules in the vertical dimension. Common information can lead to inconsistency across vertically related DW fragments. The effect of this inconsistency is felt as loss of business control.

A. **Inconsistency**

The effect of inconsistent data is seen when the refresh times of the Data Warehouse fragments, DWF, are different. Let requirements granule from PER DWFper be RGp_1 and the operations Data Warehouse DWFop be RGo_2. Let these contain overlapping information I and to distinguish between I in RGp1 and I in RGo2, I_1 and I_2 shall be used, respectively. Let it be that at ETL time of DWFper and DWFop, $I_1 = I_2 = I$. Now, let the refresh times of the two pieces of information be T_1 and T_2, respectively. Then, at T_1, I_1 changes to I'_1 whereas it is only at T_2 that I_2 changes to I'_2 to make $I'_1 = I'_2$. Thus, in the time interval $(T_2 - T_1)$, the two warehouse fragments show inconsistent values of I.

This leads to data obtained from one DW fragment to be different from that obtained in the other in the window $(T_2 - T_1)$. Thus, enforcement rule formulators and operational decision-makers end up taking decisions on different data in this temporal window. The larger this window, the longer this inconsistency exists.

That this only happens in the window makes the inconsistency problem worse than if it were to happen uniformly. It is not possible to get to the source of the problem once the second DW fragment, DWFop, has been refreshed. Thus, the problem is unrepeatable outside this window and may either go completely undetected or, if detected, the reason for the inconsistency may be difficult to find.

There is no guarantee that the two DW fragments shall be refreshed at the same time. Further, the operational level DW fragment is likely to be refreshed more frequently than that dealing with formulation of policy enforcement rules. This is because operational decision-making occurs more frequently than decision-making for rules. Therefore, given operational pressures, operational DW fragment is more likely to be kept refreshed than the rules of formulation DW fragment.

Let us examine the effect of differing refresh times and show the existence of inconsistency. Consider Table 6.5 that shows transactions and DW fragments refresh being carried out at different times.

Before the first transaction is executed, let the number of nurses in the hospital be 50. The first three rows of Table 6.5 show the deletion of three nurses from the transactional system. At Tk, the operational data warehouse fragment, DWFop, is refreshed and the number of nurses in this fragment is 47. Between Tk and Tn, DWFper continues to show that there are 50 nurses. At this moment, the data warehouse fragments are inconsistent.

Similarly, the table shows that there is inconsistency again at Tn. At To, a new nurse is added. At Tn, DWFper is refreshed and it contains 48 nurses; DWFop contains 47.

B. Loss of Business Control

Inconsistency of data in PER and operations DW fragments results in loss of business control. Consider the inconsistent information window $(T_2 - T_1)$. Three cases arise:

(a) The operations DW fragment, DWFop, is refreshed and contains latest data. This data is **not** in accordance with the policy enforcement rules governing it. Evidently, either business operations are not in conformity with the enforcement rules and there is need for better control on the operational business or the

Table 6.5 Transactions and refresh times for DWFop and DWFper

Time	Transaction	DWFop	DWFper
T1	Delete nurse$_1$		
T2	Delete nurse$_2$		
T3	Delete nurse$_3$		
Tk		Refresh	
To	Add nurse$_4$		
Tn			Refresh

business environment has changed and enforcement rules need to be reformulated.

(b) As before, DWFop is refreshed and contains the latest data. This data **is in** accordance with policy enforcement rules. Evidently, this is a benign case compared to (a): even though the data is different there is no conflict between PER and operations people.

(c) The PER DW fragment, DWFper, is refreshed and contains latest data. Therefore, PER formulators are ahead of business operations in so far as formulating rules are concerned. They may formulate new rules that operations people believe are not needed. Again, this is not a serious problem and will sort itself out once the operations DW fragment is refreshed.

As mentioned above, the operations DW fragment is more likely to be refreshed than the PER DW fragment, making case (a) a live possibility. To make case (a) precise, loss of business control occurs when data of a DW fragment from a lower level (DWFop) calls for decision-makers of the DW fragment of a higher level (DWFper) to take decisions, but the decisions are not taken because data in the latter do not suggest this need.

The two problems are illustrated using the following example. Let there be a policy "bed: nurse ratio must be 8:1". Consider a unit in a hospital consisting of 400 beds. According to the policy, the number of nurses must be 50.

The policy enforcement rule for this policy says that if the ratio falls below 8:1, then an alert to recruit new nurses is sent out; if it is greater, then an alert about excess staffing is sent out. Operational information keeps track of the number of nurses, beds, patients registered, discharged, etc.

Loss of business control occurs in the presence of DW fragment inconsistency. Recall that loss of business control occurs when DWFop may ask for a change of policy enforcement rule but DWFper may show no such need.

Consider Table 6.6. DWFop and DWFper at time T show that the hospital has the required number of nurses that is 50. At time t', DWFop shows 35 nurses whereas DWFper continues to show 50.

Consider a possible reaction by decision-makers charged with formulating rules, under the assumption that DWFper shows 50 instead of 35. Clearly, there is failure to recruit enough new nurses as required by the rule. Therefore, a new rule is required "if number of nurses is less than 80% of the required number then transfer nurses from other units".

Table 6.6 shows that DWFop is suggesting the need for a change in a policy enforcement rule but DWFper does not. Thus, loss of business control occurs since appropriate decision-making is inhibited.

Table 6.6 Data at time T and t' for DWFop and DWFper	Time	DWFop	DWFper
	T	Number of nurses = 50	Number of nurses = 50
	t'	Number of nurses = 35	Number of nurses = 50

6.8 Approaches to Consolidation

Recall that the data warehouse community has proposed data mart integration for unifying data marts into one consolidated data warehouse. As a result, different schemas are integrated and differences in data are sorted out.

In considering DW fragment integration, name conflicts are assumed to be resolved. That is, it is ensured that there is no confusion in which name refers to what concept. For example, all are agreed that employee means the same kind of employee. Now, since integration is for data model only, it is only interesting to take up the multidimensional models and integrate facts and dimensions. A number of approaches for matching facts and dimensions of data marts have been reported:

- It was demonstrated [1] that drill across operations performed over non-conforming dimensions and facts are either not possible or produce invalid results. The authors assumed that data marts are available in a variety of forms, DB2, Oracle, SQL server, etc. and proposed an integration strategy of three steps consisting of a (a) semi-automated part [2] to identify dimension compatibility, (b) verification of compatible dimensions, and (c) making incompatible dimensions compatible. Thus, the integration problem is a semantic issue.
- The approach of [3] is based on the observation that in many practical situations, the assumption that in aggregation hierarchies, levels, and their inter-relationships are given does not hold. They infer these levels and inter-relationships from their data and use them for integration.
- Golfarelli [4] positions fact/dimension conformity in the larger context of the functional and physical architecture of the integrated DW and resolution of the trade-off between technical and user priorities.
- In ORE [5], information requirements of the integrated DW are determined as a matrix of facts and dimensions. Each fact row is considered to be an information requirement and is to be realized in a single data mart. Thus, one gets as many data marts as the number of fact rows in the matrix. This collection of data marts is then integrated into the full DW by fact matching, dimension matching, exploring new multidimensional design, and final integration.

  The authors propose to use ontology for available data sources to identify relationship between concepts.

The underlying assumptions behind work on data mart integration [2] are as follows:

(a) Data marts are structured in a uniform way; they use notions of facts and dimensions only.
(b) Data quality in a data mart is usually higher than in a database because of the ETL process.

Therefore, the interesting issue is to integrate facts and dimensions across data marts for the purpose of providing a single logical schema for querying.

However, as stated in Chap. 3, these approaches are in violation of agile principle of incremental and iterative development. For this, consolidation must be done at the requirements granule stage and not left to the DW fragment level.

6.9   Consolidating Requirements Granules

It is clear that requirements granules must be consolidated in order to mitigate the problems arising due to common information. The input to the consolidation process is a pair of requirement granules. Consolidation is done through a five-step process as discussed below:

Early Information Reader

The early information reader assumes that early information (EI) is available and presents the EI of the two requirements granules, RG1 and RG2, to the correspondence drafter.

Early information reader assumes that a trace of the information obtained during requirements engineering is available. Along with the early information, EI, the reader also retrieves the following data:

- Traceability factor (TF): In the event of integrating across levels of the continuum, it is possible that a lower level requirement can be traced to a higher level requirement. This is captured in the traceability factor (TF), that is, Boolean valued. If integration is applied within a decision level, then TF is irrelevant. This is reflected in the following by setting TF by default to TRUE.
- Analysis type: analysis method used for eliciting early information, ENDSI, MEANSI, and CSFI;
- Analysis value: effectiveness measure for ENDSI, efficiency measure for MEANSI, and CSFI factor for CSFI analysis; and finally
- Early Information: early information identifier.

This can be visualized as in Table 6.7. It can be seen that the requirements granule has information for elements (rules) R1 and R2. Further, it can be seen that CSFI analysis yielded $EI_{R1,CSFI,A}$, $EI_{R1,CSFI,B}$, and using ENDSI analysis yielded $EI_{R1,ENDSI,C}$, whereas analysis of R2 yielded $EI_{R2,CSFI,D}$.

The structure of a requirements granule at the operational decision-making level is similar to the structure shown in Table 6.7. Since decisions are traceable to rules, TF is TRUE. For purposes of visualization, there is an additional column called

Table 6.7 Trace information of a requirements granule at the PER formulation decision level

Element	Analysis type	Analysis value	Early information
R1	CSFI	A	$EI_{R1,CSFI,A}$
	CSFI	B	$EI_{R1,CSFI,B}$
	ENDSI	C	$EI_{R1,ENDSI,C}$
R2	CSFI	D	$EI_{R2,CSFI, D}$

Table 6.8 Trace information of decisions

Element	Traceable to element	TF	Analysis type	Analysis value	Early information
D1	R1	TRUE	CSFI	P	$EI_{D1,CSFI,P}$
	R1		ENDSI	Q	$EI_{D1,ENDSI,Q}$
D2	R2	TRUE	CSFI	R	$EI_{D2,CSFI,R}$

traceable to rule which is the rule identifier. An example is shown in Table 6.8. Here, two decisions D1 and D2 are traceable to R1 and R2, respectively. Again, the information obtained for each decision under different analysis types is available. Here, TF is set to TRUE since D1 and D2 are traceable to PER R1 and R2, respectively.

Correspondence Drafter

The aim of the correspondence drafter is to propose candidate EI for integration to the information mapper. The correspondence drafter can be based on a number of strategies, from the brute force strategy to strong correspondence strategy. These strategies are described below:

1. **Brute Force strategy**: In this strategy, each row of EI of requirements granule, RG1, is compared with every other row of EI of RG2. For less number of comparisons, this strategy is suitable.
2. **Weak correspondence strategy (WCS)**: As the number of comparisons with the brute force strategy becomes large, there is a need to deploy heuristics. Consider early information EIR and EID. EIR and EID correspond to one another provided TF = TRUE. Thus, for Tables 6.7 and 6.8, the weak correspondences are shown in Table 6.9.
   Assuming that the amount of EI of a rule and that for a decision derived from it is not large, this strategy is suitable.
3. **Average correspondence strategy (ACS)**: As the early information to be considered in the WCS rises, there is need for a stronger heuristic. Formally, let there be two elements say R and D; analysis types AT1 as well as AT2; and early information $EI_{R,AT1}$ and $EI_{D,AT2}$. ACS says that $EI_{R,AT1}$ and $EI_{D,AT2}$ correspond to one another provided (i) TF is TRUE, and (ii) AT1 = AT2. Thus, for Tables 6.7 and 6.8, the average correspondences are shown in Table 6.10. Assuming that the amount of EI of an analysis type is not very large, this strategy is suitable.
4. **Strong correspondence strategy (SCS)**: Again, as the amount of early information to be considered in ACS rises, there is need for an even stronger heuristic. Let there be a elements R and D; analysis types and values AT1, V1 as well as AT2, V2 respectively; and early information $EI_{R,AT1,V1}$ and $EI_{D,AT2,V2}$. Now, a strong correspondence occurs between $EI_{R,AT1,V1}$ and $EI_{D,AT2,V2}$ provided (i) TF is TRUE, (ii) AT1 = AT2, and (iii) EQV(V1, V2). EQV is defined as follows:

Table 6.9 Weak correspondence strategy

DWFper	DWFop
$EI_{R1,CSFI,A}$ $EI_{R1,CSFI,B}$ $EI_{R1,ENDSI,C}$	$EI_{D1,CSFI,P}$ $EI_{D1,ENDSI,Q}$
$EI_{R2,CSFI, D}$	$EI_{D2,CSFI,R}$

Table 6.10 Average correspondence strategy

DWFper	DWFop
$EI_{R1,CSFI,A}$ $EI_{R1,CSFI,B}$	$EI_{D1,CSFI,P}$
$EI_{R1,ENDSI,C}$	$EI_{D1,ENDSI,Q}$
$EI_{R2,CSFI, D}$	$EI_{D2,CSFI,R}$

- For AT1 = AT2 = CSFI, EQV(V1, V2) if V1 is computed from V2 or V1 = V2.
- For AT1 = AT2 = ENDSI, EQV(V1, V2) if achievement of V1 contributes to achievement of V2 or V1 = V2.
- For AT1 = AT2 = MEANSI, EQV(V1, V2) if V1 is a MEANSI that contributes to the MEANSI used to achieve V2 or V1 = V2.

Assume EQV(A, P), EQV(C, Q), and EQV(D, R). Thus, for Tables 6.7 and 6.8, the strong correspondences are shown in Table 6.11. Notice that the second row shows no strong correspondence for $EI_{R1,CSFI,B}$.

Information Mapper

Once the correspondence drafter reports the correspondences, attention shifts to a more detailed examination of early information. The notion of early information was elaborated in Chap. 5 and had the following properties:

- Attribute,
- History: Whether or not its history is to be maintained,
- Categorization, and
- Function: use of a function like Count, Max, Min, etc.

To establish a mapping between correspondences generated by the correspondence drafter, there is a need to ensure that information of one can be mapped to that of the other. This is the job of the information mapper: it compares two pieces of early information, EI1 and EI2, and reports their integration, $EI_{integrated}$.

Suppose EI1 has I1, A1, H1, C1, F1 and EI2 has I2, A2, H2, C2, F2 representing information, attribute, category, and function of EI1 and EI2, respectively. While comparing EI1 and EI2, three possibilities can arise. EI1 and EI2 can be

Table 6.11 Strong correspondence strategy

DWFper	DWFop
$EI_{R1,CSFI,A}$	$EI_{D1,CSFI,P}$
$EI_{R1,CSFI,B}$	
$EI_{R1,ENDSI,C}$	$EI_{D1,ENDSI,Q}$
$EI_{R2,CSFI, D}$	$EI_{D2,CSFI,R}$

- Fully mapped: This is the case when I1 == I2 and A1 == A2, H1 == H2, C1 == C2, T1 == T2 and F1 == F2. In this case, EI1 = EI2 = EI$_{integrated}$. One copy of early information is included in EI$_{integrated}$.
- Partially mapped, if I1 == I2 and at least one of the other properties is not equal. In this case, there are conflicts that need to be examined and resolved.
- Not mapped: defined as I1 <> I2. Here, there is no overlap between the information and EI$_{integrated}$ = EI1 U EI2.

Conflict Resolver

EI which is partially mapped is sent to the conflict resolver. There are the following two kinds of conflicts.

1. Property present in EI1 and not present in EI2 or vice versa: When such a conflict arises, then the proposed heuristic is to maintain property in EI$_{integrated}$. For example, EI1 shows that history is required and EI2 shows that it is not. Obviously, then, history in EI$_{integrated}$ has to be maintained. The requirement of DW fragment DWF2 shall be satisfied with current data and that of DWF1 by current plus historical data.
2. Property present in both EI1 and EI2 but with different property values: Table 6.12 shows the different scenarios that can arise. Notice in the case of attribute, categorization, and function, EI$_{integrated}$ contains A1 U A2, C1 U C2, and F1 U F2. In the case of temporal unit, the value having the lower grain is chosen, since roll-up operations can always be performed at the level of BI tools.

Integrated information collator

At this stage, integrated early information is available for each correspondence (row) produced by the correspondence drafter. That is for each correspondence c1, c2, ... cn, we get integrated early information, EIc1, EIc2, ..., EIcn. It is possible that there may be information about the same entity in EIci and EIcj. The Collator takes the union of this information. The result of the Collator is the early information that defines the contents of the integrated DW to-be.

In conclusion, early information reader reads early information of the two requirements granules to be integrated. Correspondence drafter proposes correspondences between rules and decisions traceable to their rules. This can be done using the proposed heuristics for either brute force, WCS, ACS, or SCS strategies. Now, for each correspondence, EI is examined by the information mapper to generate EI$_{integrated}$. For this, the mapper applies heuristics to find if two given EI

Table 6.12 Conflict resolution

Property	EI1	EI2	EI$_{integrated}$
Attribute	A1	A2	Both A1 and A2
History	H1	H2	Lower grain
Categorization	C1	C2	Both C1 and C2
Function	F1	F2	Both F1 and F2

are fully mapped, partially mapped, or not mapped. Partially mapped ones move to the conflict resolution stage.

Once the requirements have been integrated, the integrated early information is converted to ER diagram and subsequently into multidimensional structures. For this, we rely on existing techniques of [6, 7].

6.9.1 An Example Showing Consolidation

Consider two requirements granules one for a rule as the element and the other for an operational decision as the element. The two elements are as follows:

Element 1   WHEN start x IF !area(x, 200) THEN expand x
Element 2   Remodel x

where range variable is <private ward> <x>.

Applying the five-step pair-wise consolidation process:

1. Early Information Reader

Consider the output of the early information reader for requirements granule of element R1 as shown in Table 6.13. Each row gives information about the element, analysis type applied, analysis value obtained, and EI identifier. Observe from Table 6.13 that EI was elicited using two CSFI factors, three ENDSI, and three MEANSI analyses. Details of the early information in the last column of Table 6.13 are provided later when we consider information mapper because these details are needed then.

Similar to Table 6.13, the next table, Table 6.14 shows the output of reading the requirements granule of element D1. There is an additional column that shows the

Table 6.13 Trace information of requirements granule for R1

S. No.	Element	Analysis type	Analysis value	Early information
1	R1	CSFI	Patient satisfaction	$EI_{R1,CSFI,PS}$
2	R1	CSFI	Quality care	$EI_{R1,CSFI,QualC}$
3	R1	ENDSI	Service higher income group patients	$EI_{R1,ENDSI,IncGrp}$
4	R1	ENDSI	Service more patients	$EI_{R1,ENDSI,Spat}$
5	R1	ENDSI	Improve patient care	$EI_{R1,ENDSI,PC}$
6	R1	MEANSI	Construct new	$EI_{R1,MEANSI,NewRoom}$
7	R1	MEANSI	Hire room	$EI_{R1,MEANSI,HireRoom}$
8	R1	MEANSI	Remodel existing Room	$EI_{R1,MEANSI,RemodRoom}$

Table 6.14 Trace information of requirements granule for D1

S. No.	Element	Traceable to element	TF	Analysis type	Analysis value	Early information
1	D1	R1	TRUE	CSFI	Patient satisfaction	EI$_{D1,CSFI,PatSat}$
2	D1	R1		CSFI	Quality care	EI$_{D1,CSFI,QC}$
3	D1	R1		ENDSI	Attract higher income group patients	EI$_{D1,ENDSI,Income}$
4	D1	R1		ENDSI	Provide patient attention	EI$_{D1,ENDSI,PatAtt}$
5	D1	R1		MEANSI	Construct new	EI$_{D1,MEANSI,NewPvt}$
6	D1	R1		MEANSI	Hire existing	EI$_{D1,MEANSI,HirePvt}$
7	D1	R1		MEANSI	Splitting room	EI$_{D1,MEANSI,SplitPvt}$
8	D1	R1		MEANSI	Adding section	EI$_{D1,MEANSI,AddSec}$

PER from which the decision is derived. Also, observe for D1, EI was elicited using two CSFI factors, two ENDSI, and four MEANSI analyses. Again, details of early information are considered when dealing with information mapper.

2. **Correspondence Drafter**

The next step is to find correspondences between each row of Tables 6.13 and 6.14. The brute force strategy when applied made the total number of comparisons also large as the EI to be consolidated was large.

Applying WCS:
WCS says that EI$_R$ and EI$_D$ correspond to one another provided

(i) TF is TRUE.

Table 6.14 shows that D1 is traceable to R1. There is a weak correspondence between EI of Tables 6.13 and 6.14. The result is shown in Table 6.15. Note that neither is the analysis type nor is the analysis value taken into consideration while drafting correspondence.

Applying ACS:
ACS says that EI$_{R,AT1}$ and EI$_{D,AT2}$ correspond to one another provided

(i) TF is TRUE and
(ii) AT1 = AT2.

Consider the first and second rows of Table 6.14. Here, D1 is traceable to R1. The analysis type is CSFI. In Table 6.13, row numbers 1 and 2 have rule as R1 and analysis type as CSFI. Thus, the correspondence is ACS. Similarly, row numbers 3

Table 6.15 Correspondence between EI_R and EI_D using WCS strategy

DWFper	DWFop
$EI_{R1,CSFI,PS}$, $EI_{R1,CSFI,QualC}$	$EI_{D1,CSFI,PatSat}$, $EI_{D1,CSFI,QC}$
$EI_{R1,ENDSI,IncGrp}$, $EI_{R1,ENDSI,Spat,}$	$EI_{D1,ENDSI,Income}$, $EI_{D1,ENDSI,PatAtt}$
$EI_{R1,ENDSI,PC}$	$EI_{D1,MEANSI,NewPvt}$;
$EI_{R1,MEANSI,NewRoom}$; $EI_{R1,MEANSI,HireRoom}$;	$EI_{D1,MEANSI,HirePvt}$;
$EI_{R1,MEANSI,RemodRoom}$	$EI_{D1,MEANSI,SplitPvt}$; $EI_{D1,MEANSI,AddSec}$

Table 6.16 Correspondence between EI_R and EI_D using ACS strategy

DWFper	DWFop
$EI_{R1,CSFI,PS}$, $EI_{R1,CSFI,QualC}$	$EI_{D1,CSFI,PatSat}$, $EI_{D1,CSFI,QC}$
$EI_{R1,ENDSI,IncGrp}$, $EI_{R1,ENDSI,Spat}$, $EI_{R1,ENDSI,PC}$	$EI_{D1,ENDSI,Income}$, $EI_{D1,ENDSI,PatAtt}$
$EI_{R1,MEANSI,NewRoom}$, $EI_{R1,MEANSI,HireRoom}$, $EI_{R1,MEANSI,RemodRoom}$	$EI_{D1,MEANSI,NewPvt}$, $EI_{D1,MEANSI,HirePvt}$, $EI_{D1,MEANSI,}$ SplitPvt, $EI_{D1,MEANSI,AddSec}$

and 4 of Table 6.14 and row numbers 3, 4, and 5 of Table 6.13 have ACS between their EIs. The result is shown in Table 6.16. Notice that the analysis value is not taken into consideration here.

Applying SCS:

Consider the first row of Tables 6.13 and 6.14. Applying the rules for SCS $EI_{R1,CSF,PS}$ and $EI_{D1,CSF,PatSat}$:

(i)   TF is TRUE.
(ii) Analysis type for both is CSFI.
(iii) $EI_{R1,CSF,PS}$ has the same analysis value "patient satisfaction" as $EI_{D1,CSFI,PatSat}$. Thus, according to the rules above, there is equivalence, EQV(PS, PatSat).

All the three conditions for strong correspondences between $EI_{R1,CSFI,PS}$ and $EI_{D1,CSFI,PatSat}$ are satisfied. Similarly, for $EI_{R1,CSFI,QualC}$ and $EI_{D1,CSFI,QC}$, and for $EI_{R1,ENDSI,IncGrp}$ and $EI_{D1,ENDSI,Income}$, a strong correspondence is found and shown in the second and third rows of the table.

The fourth row of Table 6.17 shows no entry against $EI_{R1,ENDSI,SPat}$. This is because there is no equivalent analysis value found in Table 6.14.

To obtain the fifth row of Table 6.17, consider the fifth row of Table 6.13 and the fourth row of Table 6.14. Again, rules 1 and 2 are satisfied because D1 is traceable to R1 and analysis type is the same for both, that is ENDS. Notice that achievement of "Provide patient attention" contributes to achievement of "Improve patient care". Thus, there is EQV (PC, PatAtt).

	S. No.	DWFper	DWFop
Table 6.17 Correspondence between EI_R and EI_D using SCS strategy	1	$EI_{R1,CSFI,PS}$	$EI_{D1,CSFI,PatSat}$
	2	$EI_{R1,CSFI,QualC}$	$EI_{D1,CSFI,QC}$
	3	$EI_{R1,ENDSI,IncGrp}$	$EI_{D1,ENDSI,Income}$
	4	$EI_{R1,ENDSI,Spat}$	
	5	$EI_{R1,ENDSI,PC}$	$EI_{D1,ENDSI,PatAtt}$
	6	$EI_{R1,MEANSI,NewRoom}$	$EI_{D1,MEANSI,NewPvt}$
	7	$EI_{R1,MEANSI,HireRoom}$	$EI_{D1,MEANSI,HirePvt}$
	8	$EI_{R1,MEANSI,RemodRoom}$	$EI_{D1,MEANSI,SplitPvt}$
	9	$EI_{R1,MEANSI,RemodRoom}$	$EI_{D1,MEANSI,AddSec}$

The last two entries of Table 6.17, rows 8 and 9, are obtained because the MEANS "splitting room" and "adding section" of Table 6.13 contribute to the MEANS "remodel room" of Table 6.14. Thus, there is EQV (RemodRoom, SplitPvt) and EQV (RemodRoom, AddSec).

3. Information Mapper

Information mapper checks to see if early information to be integrated is fully mapped, partially mapped, or not mapped.

Mapping Information from WCS:
The information mapper picks one EI from requirements granule of element R1 and the other from requirements granule of element D1 for integration at random. If they are fully mapped, then only one set is maintained and integrated with the next EI picked at random by the information mapper. If at any point there is a conflict, then the conflict resolver resolves the conflicts and integrates EIs. If EIs are not mapped, then both the copies are stored. This process is repeated till all the entries of Table 6.15 have been processed and integrated.

Mapping Information from ACS:
The first row of Table 6.16 has two entries from DWFper and two from DWFop. The information mapper picks one from each DWFper and DWFop at random, integrates, and then picks the remaining two for integration. After it finishes with the first row of Table 6.16, it proceeds to the second row and follows the same process. Throughout, the rules for fully mapped, partially mapped, and not mapped are followed.

Mapping Information from SCS:
Table 6.17 shows that $EI_{R1,CSFI,PS}$ and $EI_{D1,CSFI,PatSat}$ have a strong correspondence. The process of information mapping for CSFI analysis type is shown below. Consider information for $EI_{R1,CSFI,PS}$ and $EI_{D1,CSFI,PatSat}$ as shown in Table 6.18.

Clearly, information "Patient" is mapped. Now is the question of whether it is fully or partially mapped. Notice here that while patient of $EI_{R1,CSFI,PS}$ is not categorized, patient of $EI_{D1,CSFI,PatSat}$ is categorized unit-wise, ward-wise, and

Table 6.18 Early information for $EI_{R1,CSFI,PS}$ and $EI_{D1,CSFI,PatSat}$

Early information	Information	Attribute	History	Category	Function
$EI_{R1,CSFI,PS}$	Patient		Yearly		Count
$EI_{D1,CSFI,PatSat}$	Patient		Yearly	Unit-wise Ward-wise Department-wise	Count

Table 6.19 Early information after integrating $EI_{R1,CSFI,PS}$ and $EI_{D1,CSFI,PatSat}$

Information	Attribute	History	Category	Function
Patient		Yearly	Unit-wise Ward-wise Department-wise	Count

department-wise. Thus, they are partially mapped and this conflict is resolved by the conflict resolver. $EI_{integrated}$ obtained is shown in Table 6.19.

Consider information for $EI_{R1,CSFI,QualC}$ and $EI_{D1,CSFI,QC}$ shown in Table 6.20. Information disease has the same attribute, history, and category and function values in both the rows. Thus, for information disease, the EI are fully mapped.

Doctor and Patient are unique to $EI_{R1,CSFI,J}$ and not mapped. Thus, $EI_{integrated}$ obtained is shown in Table 6.21.

In the next iteration, Tables 6.20 and 6.21 are integrated, conflicts resolved and the resulting $EI_{integrated}$ is shown in Table 6.22.

This process is repeated for all the entries of Table 6.17. After $EI_{integrated}$ is obtained, this information is converted to ER diagram and then to a star schema.

Table 6.20 Early information for $EI_{R1,CSFI,QualC}$ and $EI_{D1,CSFI,QC}$

Early information	Information	Attribute	History	Category	Function
$EI_{R1,CSFI,QualC}$	Disease	Name	Monthly	Type-wise	
$EI_{D1,CSFI,QC}$	Disease Doctor Patient	Name Speciality Income	Monthly Monthly Monthly	Type-wise Daily	Count

Table 6.21 Early information after integrating $EI_{R1,CSFI,QualC}$ and $EI_{D1,CSFI,QC}$

Information	Attribute	History	Category	Function
Disease	Name	Monthly	Type-wise	
Doctor	Speciality	Monthly	Daily	
Patient	Income	Monthly		Count

Table 6.22 EI$_{integrated}$ after integrating from Tables 6.19 and 6.21

Information	Attribute	History	Category	Function
Disease	Name	Monthly	Type-wise	
Doctor	Speciality	Monthly	Daily	
Patient	Income	Monthly	Unit-wise Ward-wise Department-wise	Count

6.10 Tool Support

We have already introduced the tool Fetchit in earlier chapters. Fetchit also supports requirements granule consolation. There are four components, the early information reader, correspondence drafter, information mapper, and the conflict resolver. The architecture is shown in Figs. 6.9 and 6.10. The first two components used in the process, namely, early information reader and correspondence drafter are shown in Fig. 6.9. The architecture involving information mapper and conflict resolver is shown in Fig. 6.10.

Figure 6.9 shows that early information reader has the early information base as input. It reads the early information of the requirements granules and sends it to the correspondence drafter. The requirements engineer is presented with a list of four strategies to select from, based on which the correspondence drafter finds correspondences between the requirements granules in a pair-wise manner and stores the same.

The correspondences output from the correspondence drafter (shown in Fig. 6.9), together with the early information in the early information base, form the input to the information mapper (shown in Fig. 6.10). For each pair of information

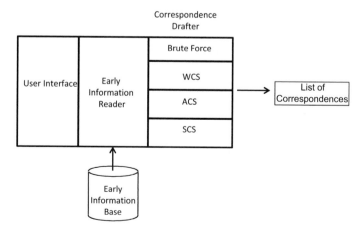

Fig. 6.9 Fetchit for determining correspondences

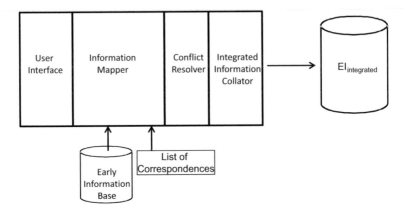

Fig. 6.10 Fetchit for consolidating early information

being integrated, the information mapper finds if it is fully, partially, or not mapped. For fully mapped information, one copy is taken into the next iteration of integration. Partially mapped information is sent to the conflict resolver. Once the conflict is resolved, one copy of the resolved information is taken into the next iteration of integration. Naturally, for not mapped information, both the pieces of information are taken into the next iteration of integration. The final set of integrated information is stored in $EI_{integrated}$ shown in Fig. 6.10.

As far as automation is concerned, no manual intervention is required in the early information reader component of Fetchit. With respect to the correspondence drafter, manual intervention is required to select a correspondence strategy. Once this is selected, correspondences are generated automatically for WCS and ACS strategies. For SCS, manual intervention is required for finding equivalence between values of the analysis types. No manual intervention is required in the information mapper component and the conflict resolver component. Thus, Fetchit is a semi-automated tool to integrate requirements granules with manual intervention required in the SCS strategy of the correspondence drafter.

Let us also examine the time taken for Fetchit to consolidate requirements granules.

Time taken for drafting correspondences: In SCS, for defining EQV(V1, V2), if the case is that V1 = V2, then the time taken to define equivalence is not high. No interaction with the requirements engineer is required as the correspondence drafter itself finds the equivalence. However, for the other cases, namely, V1 is computed from V2; V1 contributes to achievement of V2; and V1 is a means that contributes to the means used to achieve V2; EQV has to be defined by the requirements engineer. This part is a manual process and a time-taking one.

In ACS, since it is a direct text search, there is no intervention required by the requirements engineer and therefore the time taken to form correspondences is lower than SCS.

Table 6.23 Trade-off between different correspondence strategies

Correspondence Strategy	Time taken for drafting correspondences	Number of times hit to conflict resolver
WSC	Lowest	Highest
ASC	Average	Average
SCS	Highest	Lowest

In WCS, again there is no intervention required by the requirements engineer and is much faster than SCS. Between ACS and WCS, there is no significant time difference.

Number of times conflict resolver had to resolve issues: It is seen that the number of times conflicts are resolved is the lowest while employing SCS and maximum during WCS. This is because of the random nature of picking up a pair of EI for integration. By forming correspondences in ACS and SCS, the random nature of forming an EI pair is reduced. Note that there is no randomness in SCS strategy. This means that the time taken to form $EI_{integrated}$ was maximum in WCS and minimum in SCS.

The Trade-off: There is **a trade-off between time taken by the correspondence drafter and number of conflicts to be resolved**. This is shown in Table 6.23.

6.11   Conclusion

In order to make DW development agile, a model-driven technique based on the Decision Application Model, DAM, is used. This takes the development of DW user stories from an ad hoc experienced based process to a model-driven one. The model has the notion of an element at its core. An element is a generic notion and is anything about which a decision is to be taken. In our case, it can be a policy, policy formulation rule, or an operational act.

The structure and properties of a decision application are represented in the model. The instance diagram of DAM is a hierarchy of the application, decision, and information levels, respectively. The notion of a requirement changes from level to level reflecting the application, decision, and information perspectives. Vertical slicing of the hierarchy yields the requirements granules that can be taken into development. These slices are expressed as DW user stories.

DW user stories follow the Who, What, and Why structure of Scrum user stories. However, the difference is that the What part specifies the information relevant to the decision expressed as the Why part.

Since requirements granules are taken up for DW fragment development in an incremental and iterative fashion, there is the likelihood of DW fragment proliferation. The consolidation process provides different strategies of consolidation depending on the nature of the consolidation problem. Since consolidation of requirements granules is carried out, our consolidation process is a subprocess of the requirements engineering stage.

References

1. Cabibbo, L., & Torlone, R. (2004, June). On the integration of autonomous data marts. In *16th International Conference on Scientific and Statistical Database Management, 2004. Proceedings* (pp. 223–231). IEEE.
2. Cabibbo, L., Panella, I., Torlone, R., & Tre, U. R. (2006, April). DaWaII: A tool for the integration of autonomous data marts. In *ICDE* (p. 158).
3. Riazati, D., Thom, J. A., & Zhang, X. (2010, January). Inferring aggregation hierarchies for integration of data marts. In *Database and expert systems applications* (pp. 96–110). Berlin: Springer.
4. Golfarelli, M., Rizzi, S., & Turricchia, E. (2011). Modern software engineering methodologies meet data warehouse design: 4WD. In *Data warehousing and knowledge discovery* (pp. 66–79). Berlin: Springer.
5. Jovanovic, P., Romero, O., Simitsis, A., Abelló, A., & Mayorova, D. (2014). A requirement-driven approach to the design and evolution of data warehouses. *Information Systems, 44,* 94–119.
6. Golfarelli, M., Maio, D., & Rizzi, S. (1998, January). Conceptual design of data warehouses from E/R schemes. In *Proceedings of the Thirty-First Hawaii International Conference on System Sciences,* 1998 (Vol. 7, pp. 334–343). IEEE.
7. Moody, L. D., & Kortink, M. A. R. (2000). From enterprise models to dimensional models: A methodology for data warehouses and data mart design. In *Proceednigs of the International Workshop on Design and Management of Data Warehouses* (pp. 5.1–5.12). Stockholm, Sweden.

Chapter 7
Conclusion

From a global standpoint, this book has presented an approach to the unification of (a) agile methods in data warehouse development, (b) data warehouse consolidation, and (c) data warehouse requirements engineering. This is in contrast to the traditional attitude of the data warehouse community to these issues. Data warehouse developers consider data warehouse development methods, data mart consolidation, and data warehouse requirements engineering as three separate problems. To elaborate:

1. Agile development strategies for data warehouse development concentrate on cutting down product delivery times. The backlog of user stories leads to proliferation of product increments that are to be consolidated. However, techniques for consolidation like merge with primary do not find mention in agile methods. Thus, consolidation does not seem to be of direct concern in agile methods.

   Agile data warehouse development methods also do not, by and large, take into account results obtained in the area of data warehouse requirements engineering. The agile community still believes that requirements engineering produces monolithic specifications and has not investigated the possibility of obtaining requirements of product increments from requirements engineering processes in an agile manner. In fact, in agile development, requirements of product increments are obtained by techniques that are specific to the individual agile process used. These techniques are interview based, are not model-driven, and rely overly on the experience of the product owner and the development team.

2. Consolidation is merely a consequence of the incremental and iterative development processes adopted and it lies completely outside the development process. It is only when users face problems due to data mart proliferation that the consolidation process kicks in. Approaches for consolidation therefore do not impact data warehouse development methods. The world of consolidation processes and that of development processes are isolated from one another.

© Springer Nature Singapore Pte Ltd. 2018
N. Prakash and D. Prakash, *Data Warehouse Requirements Engineering*,
https://doi.org/10.1007/978-981-10-7019-8_7

The focus of consolidation is on reaching a common data model and a common platform to provide a single version of the truth. During consolidation, the question as to what are the requirements of the consolidated product is not even asked and the focus is on integrating data models. Thus, it is assumed that the requirements of the consolidated data mart are met by an integration of data models. No investigation is carried out to identify any new requirements thrown up by the subject area of the consolidated data mart.

3. Data warehouse requirements engineering concentrates on determining the requirements specification of the data warehouse to be taken into development. The assumption is that requirements of the entire data warehouse product are to be produced. It can be seen that this approach supports monolithic data warehouse development well. However, when it comes to addressing incremental and iterative development, then this requirements engineering approach fails. Indeed, there seems to be little, if any, research into determining the boundaries of product increments. Similarly, there has not been enough investigation in defining concepts that shall form the basis for requirements engineering of product increments.

The lack of interest in developing requirements increments, perhaps, also explains that the requirements engineering community has not considered the problem of requirements consolidation. After all, if there are no increments to be integrated and only a full requirements specification is to be made, then there is nothing to integrate. Therefore, the consolidation problem does not even arise.

In integrating the three areas of data warehouse requirements engineering, consolidation, and agile development, we notice that at the core of unification lies in the issue of requirements of increments. Once requirements of the product increment are determined, then development can proceed. These increment requirements can follow the 80–20 approach of Scrum user stories, backlog of data stories of BEAM*, or the specification approach for data marts. Nevertheless, some statement of requirements is needed.

Similarly, requirements also lie at the heart of consolidation. Whereas a system can be analyzed by breaking it up into its components, its synthesis is not merely the collection of its components. The "sticking glue" that allows combination of the components is needed. This means that integration of increment requirements into a new requirements increment shall not be enough and there might be missing requirements.

We refer to the requirements of a data warehouse increment as a requirements granule. Evidently, the size of a requirements granule has to be carefully determined. From the perspective of strategic alignment, maximum benefit shall be gained if business needs and priorities and the requirements granule are properly aligned. From the IT perspective, the larger the size of the requirements granule, the greater is the lead time for delivery. On the other hand, intuitively speaking, large-sized granule leads to lesser need for consolidation.

A requirements granule identifies the information that shall go into a data warehouse fragment. This expression is made as early information, obtained from the proposed suite of four techniques, and subsequently structured into multidimensional form. Thus, a requirements granule can be taken into development and yields a data warehouse fragment.

Consolidation of data warehouse fragments flows from integration of requirements granules. Requirements integration looks for the missing glue between granules being integrated. Since a consolidated requirements granule is being made, requirements of the consolidated increment are to be developed. Existing requirements granules going into the increment only contribute to these and do not entirely define these requirements.

Consolidation of requirements granules not only leads naturally to a consolidated data model but it also naturally leads to data warehouse fragments residing on a common platform. This follows from unification of the consolidation process with the requirements engineering process. Whenever requirements engineering is done, an attempt is made to consolidate existing requirements granules. This requires a centralization of granules and no granule, except the first, can be built unless an attempt at consolidation is made. This centralization in an organization facilitates use of a single platform and is a natural deterrent to multiple platforms.

The agile data warehouse development process resulting from the foregoing is shown in Fig. 7.1. The requirements engineering process subsumes consolidation in it and produces a requirements granule. This granule is then taken into conceptual design and the resulting multidimensional design, Granular MD Design, is then taken into the construction step. The result is a data warehouse fragment, DW Fragment, for the requirements granule.

The requirement engineering process itself is decision-centric. That is, instead of starting out with statements like "we wish to analyze sales" and then reaching the information required to do this analysis, the decision-centric approach starts off with decisions like "we wish to stop erosion of customer base" and then determining information that is relevant to this decision. Determining decisions is therefore the key.

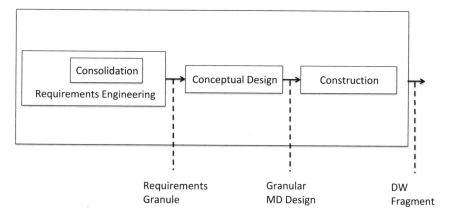

Fig. 7.1 The agile data warehouse development process

Fig. 7.2 Obtaining decisions

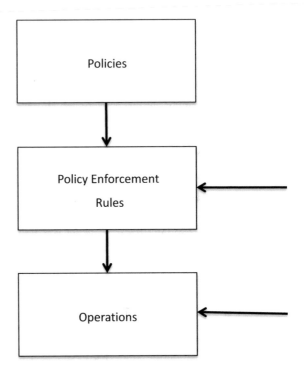

There are two ways in which decisions can be determined, by horizontal entry or by vertical entry. This is shown in Fig. 7.2. Vertical entry refers to using the stack of three types of decisions, policy, policy enforcement rules, and operational, thereby exploiting the relationship across them. That is, decisions are obtained for formulating a policy, then determining its enforcement rules and formulating decisions for selection of appropriate rules, and finally formulating operational decisions.

Horizontal entry refers to selecting the level directly. This is done when

(a) Policies are given and support for enforcement rules is required. The policy level is ignored and the requirements engineer enters into the policy enforcement rules level as shown by the horizontal arrow in Fig. 7.2.
(b) Interest is only in operational decisions. In this situation, direct entry can be made into the operations level as shown in Fig. 7.2.

Having obtained the decision(s) of interest, the next task is that of eliciting information for each. There are four techniques for doing this. All of these have stakeholder buy-in and, when used as a suite of techniques, the possibility of missing information is mitigated.

The decision-centric approach provides a unit around which the entire requirements engineering process can be developed. This unit is specific; it is a decision that is required to be taken in an organization and is an alternative of the choice set. Elicitation of decisions is a part of the requirements engineering process.

The unitary nature of a decision is exploited in elicitation of relevant information. Information elicitation techniques are deployed for each decision and thereafter a conceptual schema is built for the elicited information. This is subsequently carried through to construction of a data warehouse fragment.

The unitary role played by a decision facilitates agility in data warehouse development. This is because development can be taken up decision-wise. If the entire requirements granule relevant to a decision is considered too large to be taken into development, then a data warehouse fragment for a subset of this granule, rather than for the full granule, is developed. This provides for faster delivery but compromises on the extent of support provided by the fragment for the decision. Information for the missing part of the requirements granule is either obtained through manual systems or, if not obtained at all, the decision-making task relies more heavily on decision-maker judgment.